SPAIN'S CIVIL

D0143634

Spain's Civil War

SECOND EDITION

HARRY BROWNE

LONGMAN
LONDON AND NEW YORK

Addison Wesley Longman Limited
Edinburgh Gate,
Harlow, Essex CM20 2JE,
United Kingdom
and Associated Companies throughout the world

*Published in the United States of America
by Addison Wesley Longman, New York*

First published 1983
Second edition 1996

ISBN 0 582 289882

British Library Cataloguing in Publication Data

A catalogue record for this book is available from the British Library

Library of Congress Cataloging-in-Publication Data

Browne, Harry, 1918–
Spain's Civil War / Harry Browne. -- 2nd ed.
    p.   cm. -- (Seminar studies in history)
Includes bibliographical references (p.   ) and index.
ISBN 0-582-28988-2 (ppr)
1. Spain--History--Civil War, 1936–1939. I. Title. II. Series.
DP269.B83 1996
946.081--dc20
                                                                96-16745
                                                                CIP

Set by 7 in Sabon
Produced through Longman Malaysia, CLP

CONTENTS

Editorial foreword   vii
Note on referencing system   vii
Acknowledgements   viii
Map 1: Regions of Spain   x
Map 2: Major areas of political affiliation under the Republic   xii

PART ONE: THE BACKGROUND   1

1. INTRODUCTION   1

2. THE SECOND REPUBLIC, 1931–36   8
    The Azaña reforms   8
    The Sanjurjada, 1932   13
    The insurrection of 1934   15
    Politics and parties on the eve of the Civil War   19
    The Popular Front   29
    The Republic in danger   32

PART TWO: THE CIVIL WAR, 1936–39   37

3. THE MILITARY RISING   37

4. THE INTERNATIONALISATION OF THE WAR   48

5. THE REPUBLIC – OR THE REVOLUTION?   54

6. THE USE OF TERROR   63

7. A NEW BEGINNING – OR OLD-STYLE MILITARY
    AUTOCRACY?   66

8. THE MILITARY CAMPAIGNS   71

9. INTERNATIONAL AID   77

10. THE REPUBLIC UNDER NEGRÍN   85

PART THREE: ASSESSMENT   89

11. RETROSPECT   89

12. THE LEGACY OF THE CIVIL WAR   95
    Spain and the world outside   95
    The effects on Spain   97

PART FOUR: DOCUMENTS   103

Political personalities   131
Glossary and abbreviations   133
Bibliography   135
Index   142

EDITORIAL FOREWORD

Such is the pace of historical enquiry in the modern world that there is an ever-widening gap between the specialist article or monograph, incorporating the results of current research, and general surveys, which inevitably become out of date. *Seminar Studies in History* are designed to bridge this gap. The books are written by experts in their field who are not only familiar with the latest research but have often contributed to it. They are frequently revised, in order to take account of new information and interpretations. They provide a selection of documents to illustrate major themes and provoke discussion, and also a guide to further reading. Their aim is to clarify complex issues without over-simplifying them, and to stimulate readers into deepening their knowledge and understanding of major themes and topics.

ROGER LOCKYER

NOTE ON REFERENCING SYSTEM

Readers should note that numbers in square brackets [5] refer them to the corresponding entry in the Bibliography at the end of the book (specific page references are given in italics). A number in square brackets preceded by *Doc.* [*Doc.* 5] refers readers to the corresponding item in the Documents section which follows the main text. Words which are defined in the Glossary are asterisked on their first occurrence in the book.

ACKNOWLEDGEMENTS

The publishers would like to thank the following for permission to reproduce copyright material: Sheed and Ward for an extract from *Correspondent in Spain*, by H. Edward Knoblaugh; Jonathan Cape for an extract from *Jose Antonio Primo de Rivera, Selected Writings*, by Hugh Thomas; Freedom Press for an extract from *Collectives in the Spanish Revolution*, by Gaston Leval; Faber and Faber Ltd for an extract from *Crusade in Spain*, by Jason Gurney; Victor Gollancz for an extract from *What I Saw in Spain*, by Dame Leah Manning; Fontana, an imprint of HarperCollins Publishers Limited for an extract from *Franco*, by Paul Preston; Reed Consumer Books Ltd for extracts from *The Civil War in Spain* by Robert Payne published by Secker & Warburg, 1969.

Whilst every effort has been made to trace the owners of copyright material, in a few cases this has proved to be problematic and so we take this opportunity to offer our apologies to any copyright holders whose rights we may have unwittingly infringed.

MAPS

Map 1 Regions and provinces of Spain

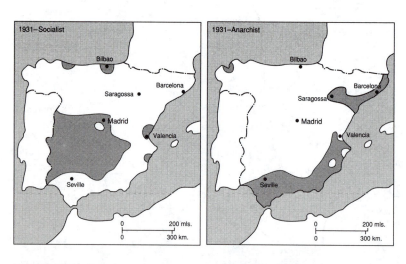

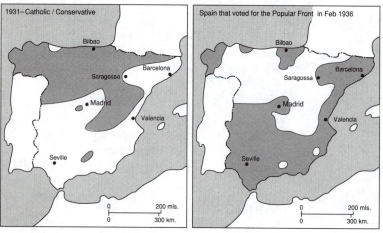

Map 2   Major areas of political affiliation under the Republic
Source: G. Brenan, The Spanish Labyrinth, Cambridge University Press

PART ONE: THE BACKGROUND

1 INTRODUCTION

Since the beginning of the nineteenth century, Spain has suffered a series of civil wars of which that of the 1930s – to all outside Spain *the* Civil War – is the most recent and certainly the most crippling in terms of simple human and material loss. Fundamentally Spanish in origin, these were wars between town and country, between constitutionalists and Carlists, between new and old Spain. Sometimes, as in the wars of the 1830s or 1930s, foreigners were drawn in to what were essentially domestic conflicts between Spaniards with differing visions of Spain. The war of 1936–39 fell within this long, unhappy tradition: it was fought with the ferocity of Carlist* wars, and, on the Nationalist side, with the banners and slogans of Old Castile, defending herself against the new insidious poison of Marxism. The Church and the Catholic middle class fought the war as a crusade against godless ideas threatening the true quality of Spanish life and they rallied enthusiastically behind the army leaders who raised their standard in a traditional *pronunciamiento.** On both sides the war began with a simple panoply of ideas: defence of the Republic pitted against a call to restore public order. In Europe, the Spanish war was quickly confused with the fascist challenge to democracy, and Spanish problems were interpreted in European terms; yet, in fact, the breakdown had peculiarly Spanish causes. Indeed, it might almost be seen as a consequence of Spain's failure to become a mature state rather than as evidence of her involvement with the major European conflicts of the 1930s. In the view of one Spanish historian, Carlos Rama [18], the Civil War resulted from Spain's failure to create a state which could command at least the allegiance, and perhaps even the lukewarm support, of its citizens.

One institution traditionally not offering more than lipservice to the state was the Army, which had seen itself as the quintessence of all that was Spanish, representing – no matter what the political system – the authentic 'general will'. This conviction that the Army *was* Spain had been demonstrated at many different times in the nineteenth century, and most recently in 1923, when the Captain General of Catalonia, General Primo de Rivera, had 'pronounced' against the parliamentary regime and established the *dictadura,** a military autocracy – even though he tried, gradually and unsuccessfully, to edge it back towards a constitutional regime, before finally resigning office in 1930. Within the Army, the most conscious of their role, and the most bitterly critical of parliamentary regimes, were the *africanistas,** officers who had served in the residual Spanish empire in Africa. In the 1936 Rising all the leaders were *africanistas,* and in this sense the rebellion may be seen not only as a military uprising but also as a colonial officers' coup against their civilian overlords in mainland Spain.

When in 1931 the Army withdrew support from Alfonso XIII, he silently packed his bags and drove off to England and exile [26]. The monarchy, by its link with Primo in 1923, had eroded its own position, and 'Enlightened' Spain, the large towns, had declared for the Republican-Socialist alliance in the municipal elections of 12 April 1931. The countryside and the small towns, however, were still overwhelmingly monarchist, which was no good harbinger for the future. In the new Republic the traditional monarchist classes – apart from a minority with the Alfonsist party, the *Renovación Española** – backed the opposition Catholic party, the *Acción Nacional** (later CEDA*). Monarchism remained in Spain as a force but without an obvious candidate, except amongst Navarrese Carlists who still nostalgically campaigned for the absent Carlos Hugo [29]. The political danger of this passive monarchism lay in its reluctant acceptance of the Second Republic: like the Right in Weimar Germany, the monarchists assumed that Republican Spain would be only an interlude in Spain's monarchical history.

Within Spain, the position of the Catholic Church had progressively weakened. Until 1808 and the popular revolt against the French invader and '*el rey intruso*', Joseph, the French-imposed king, the Church had successfully warded off attacks by ministers anxious, under the influence of the Spanish Enlightenment, to bring the Church more firmly under the control of the central government. Ministers and intellectuals [8] had tried to portray the Church as the defender of obscurantism and as largely responsible for the backwardness of Spain. These criticisms became part of the rhetoric deployed by the Cortes of 1812 against the Church, which led to the suppression of the Inquisition and the beginning of an attempt to divest the Church of her land and her wealth. Although the restoration of Ferdinand VII, following the expulsion of Joseph and the French, led to the re-establishment of the privileged status of the Church and the renewal of the Inquisition, increasingly the new liberalism came to dominate the policy of Madrid. In the 1830s a movement initiated by the Liberal Minister Mendizábal led to the expropriation of Church lands. The final outcome of this process was a Concordat between Church and State in 1851 which did at least guarantee priests an income and recognised Catholicism as the religion of Spain.

From this Concordat began, as Gerald Brenan shows [2], that fateful alliance between upper-class Spain and a Church now increasingly dependent upon the rich for additional income, and therefore isolated from the poor in town and country alike. The Church came to be seen as the Church of the wealthy, and the hierarchy as the defender of conservatism of all kinds. In the troubled times of post-First-World-War Spain, the Church offered no guidance, suggested no means by which the extremes of poverty could be reduced, was of the king's party in the 1920s and, almost without exception, of Franco's party in 1936. In the crisis of the monarchy, in 1930–31, the Church had withdrawn its support from Alfonso XIII, in common with the established classes and the traditional institutions, but the Church's attitude to the new Republic was initially no more than neutral, a neutrality which rapidly passed over into active hostility as the liberalism of the Republic's leaders revealed itself as markedly anti-clerical.

Historically, Spanish liberalism began with an attempt to frame a constitution within a society overrun by the foreigner and long subject to arbitrary government. That first attempt, the Constitution of 1812, gave a model to Europe as well as to Spain and incurred the passionate condemnation of the Spanish Church which identified liberalism with an attack upon itself [3]. The Church's over-readiness to castigate political liberalism incited in late nineteenth-century Liberals, of whom Manuel Azaña is the outstanding example, an implacable anti-clericalism. Teachers such as Francisco Giner, founder of the Institute of Free Education in 1875, tried to exclude religious influence from education by creating colleges outside the church system; anarchists like Francisco Ferrer, with his Modern School movement in Catalonia in the early 1900s, sought to offer an alternative moral system to that of Catholicism [24]. Church control of education, both in the state-supported primary and secondary schools (more an ideal than a reality) and particularly in the schools of the religious orders, allowed free play for blatantly anti-liberal doctrines. In this control reformers saw the secret of the Church's hold on Spain. Therefore, when the new Republican government, based upon a Liberal-Socialist alliance, came into office in 1931, it saw its first task as ending the Concordat and removing education from the Church. The Liberals were working within a narrow orthodoxy concerned to bring Spain into the twentieth century, and to create a constitution based upon a modernised society where religion was a matter for the individual and not for the state. The Church reacted to this as an attack upon religion, upon morality, upon the family, upon the traditional Spain by men seized of ideas fostered by freemasons and unbelievers and careless of the fundamental bases of Spanish life [42].

Just as liberalism could be seen as fracturing the mystical unity of Spain, based upon the Catholic Church, so could cultural and political regionalism appear as a threat to Spain's political unity. Regionalism and localism, the passionate loyalty to birthplace enshrined in the cult of *patria chica*,* had long been potent forces in Spain, traditions which sprang in part from a long-established anti-centralism and were nourished by the differing languages and histories of Galicia, the Basque Provinces and Catalonia. Basque and Catalan regionalism were also powered by the vital industrial and commercial traditions of these two wealthy regions, both speaking non-Castilian languages. Catalan regionalism had already been granted some recognition by the *Mancomunidad* of 1913, which grouped together for local government the four principally Catalan provinces of Barcelona, Lérida, Tarragona and Gerona. Under the dictatorship of Primo de Rivera in the 1920s, this partial recognition of the strength of Catalan regionalism had been suppressed, the Catalan language banned, and a fresh attempt made to give life to Spanish unity. Catalan cultural and linguistic pride had been severely damaged and political ambitions sharpened when Catalan nationalists framed demands for a separate state within a federated Spain. With the coming of the Republic in 1931, Catalans who had helped topple the monarchy expected political reward for their support. To conservative Spain, this seemed to be confirmation of Catalan egoism, and it was feared that what Catalonia demanded today, Basques and others would want tomorrow [1].

Catalan and Basque aspirations were buttressed by the economic progress which their regions could display. Jordi Nadal [13] has argued that in the nineteenth century Spain in general failed to take advantage of the opportunities for rapid industrial change which were on offer. Certainly, the twentieth-century economic map of

Spain showed evidence of what Sánchez-Albornoz [20] has called a 'dual economy', with areas of progress such as Catalonia and the Basque Provinces and areas of stagnation such as Andalusia. This dualism extended into agriculture as well as industry, with Valencia diversifying crops and developing citrus fruit production, and parts of Andalusia – Jaén, for example – still maintaining a single-crop economy based upon the olive.

In Catalonia, fundamentally a land of peasant proprietors, a diverse economy had been created, with textiles as the principal industry, but also extending into machine making and the highly profitable activities associated with shipping. Barcelona, the major port of Catalonia, was run by the great families, Catalan industrialists, who looked to capitalist Europe for their model and for their cultural contacts, rather than to Castile. Industrial capitalists in Catalonia had little in common with the agrarian grandees of Castile who lived content with wealth from rents and from unimproved agriculture, based often upon *latifundios*,* great landed estates with a traditional agriculture failing to provide sufficient food for Spain's population. These *latifundios* created vast pools of rural discontent, with labourers living in continual poverty, only partially employed throughout the work year. In rural Spain the contrast between rich and poor was stark; there were no people of the middling sort, few gradations of wealth and class. The new Republic inherited the problems of low agricultural productivity, landless labourers, and impoverished tenants [9; 10].

In agricultural regions such as Andalusia, Bakunin's anarchism took firm root; land-hungry peasants in the scattered villages of the South heard the promise of the new age which anarchism would bring when the day of revolution finally came [103]. Its shape was clearly defined: there would be a *reparto*, a redistribution of land; men would be equal; there would be no more grandees, no more priests, no tax gatherers and no civil guards. The means of bringing all this about was ill defined, the tactics shadowy, but come the day – so the anarchists asserted – there would be a spontaneous uprising. This certainty that the millennium would arrive made organisation unnecessary and doctrinally wrong, for each anarchist must be master of himself alone, and of no one else [99; 115; 116].

In Catalonia, in industrialised Barcelona, anarchist doctrines were modified into anarcho-syndicalism, from which developed trade unions with moderates thinking in terms of traditional trade-union objectives: a shorter working day, improved pay, and arbitration committees. On the left, however, classical anarchists were still committed to political strikes and to direct action – murder and robbery – as revolutionary tactics to hasten the birth of the new society. The industrial context of Catalonia, with the small patronal factory employing ten or a dozen men, created networks of working-class relationships profoundly different from the agricultural South and made imperative the discussion of industrial relations and short-term objectives. In Andalusia, on the other hand, anarchist objectives were necessarily long-term, for neither absentee landlords nor bailiffs were susceptible to pressures for improvement.

By 1931 the CNT* – the anarchist federation based in Catalonia and suppressed under Primo de Rivera – had re-emerged as the major left-wing movement in Spain. It was committed to a transformation of society, hostile to the democratic system, unwilling to vote or put forward parliamentary candidates. The tragedy for the Spanish Left was the hold that anarchist doctrines had upon the Spanish working class and the fatal split between the CNT and the socialist trade union (the UGT*) with its bastions of power in Madrid, Bilbao and the Asturias. The PSOE,* the political voice of the UGT, formed part of the Republican ruling coalition, but was numerically weaker than the CNT.

Spain entered the 1930s a backward state, still largely agricultural, with levels of poverty equalled only by other Mediterranean regions such as Greece or Sicily. In politics she was burdened with a newly constructed political system which called for civic loyalties which many Spaniards, deeply localist in sentiment and unused to thinking in broader terms, could in no way sustain. Furthermore, her class system was firmly etched upon the national character, with categories such as peasant, town worker, grandee, landlord, middle-class politician – divided by income, by education, and by bitter hostility. The Spanish political scene reflected these antagonisms, with parties such as *Acción Popular** representing Catholic small farmers and the PSOE the town worker. What was desperately needed was some way in which these divisions could be bridged and a common purpose established, perhaps by national reforms which would bring Spain clearly into the twentieth century. Above all, Spain needed to create more wealth to alleviate poverty, and to ensure a fairer distribution of her national goods in order to eradicate gross inequality. Was the Republic equipped to provide the leadership – or the means – by which this could be done?

In many countries in the world the economic depression of the late 1920s had profound political consequences; in England, a National Government; in America, the New Deal; in Germany, the

Nazi 'seizure of power'. The Spanish Republic was born in the middle of the world depression, but Josep Fontana and Jordi Nadal deny that this 'had a decisive effect on republican Spain' [6 *p. 485*]. The reason for Spain's relative immunity from major damage lay in the national policy for self-sufficiency which stretched back into the late nineteenth century, when a Spanish government, after a brief flirtation with free trade, returned to strict protectionism. This traditional policy was followed by the Republic in imposing high import duties on agricultural and industrial products. In 1932, for instance, Spanish sugar was cushioned behind a tariff wall of 166 per cent on its domestic price, in itself 30 per cent higher than the world price.

Spain could not escape totally unscathed from the stagnation in world trade. Her exports of goods ranging from citrus fruits to minerals dropped disastrously. Her human exports of surplus inhabitants to Latin America and to France – a traditional safety-valve – fell steadily, at a time when her population, which had grown from 18 million in 1900 to 24 million in 1930, was still rising. Emigrants had moved abroad at a steady rate of around 32,000 a year, but after 1931 many were forced to move back. By the end of 1933 more than 100,000 emigrants had returned, thereby increasing the pressure on Spain's scant resources.

One economic characteristic of the Republic was, perhaps, important in explaining the class division which 1936–39 revealed. The Republic had seen an improvement in wage rates in Spain's major industries. An analysis of mining, metallurgy, minerals and agriculture shows a rise in real incomes between 1931 and 1936 ranging from 15 to 21 per cent. Yet in the decade after the end of the Civil War the same wage rates fell to less than 50 per cent of what they had been before [6]. Although these statistics should not be allowed to bear too heavy an interpretative weight, they may suggest that the possessing classes welcomed Franco as a means of once more redressing the balance in their favour.

2 THE SECOND REPUBLIC, 1931–36

THE AZAÑA REFORMS

The elections of June 1931 gave Azaña's party, the Left Republicans, 80 seats in a Cortes* of 473, and his Socialist allies a further 120 seats, with the conservatives holding 80. In the centre stood the 'historic' Republicans, the Radical Party of Alejandro Lerroux. The new Cortes had deputies from the various regionalist parties and representatives of other minority interests, notably from the 'Generation of '98' – those intellectuals who, after the disastrous defeat in the Spanish-American war of 1898, offered explanations of the causes of Spain's collapse and pointed to the means of regeneration. On this group Ortega y Gasset and Miguel de Unamuno were prominent, both of whom became quickly disillusioned with the Republic they had helped to bring into existence.

The new constitution declared boldly that 'Spain is a republic of workers of all classes' – a slogan coined by the Socialist Luis Araquistain. The inclusion of three Socialist ministers in the government suggested that this claim could be justified. In essence, however, the Provisional Government was dominated by politicians concerned to provide Spain with a genuinely liberal constitution without disturbing the bases of social and economic power. Its political respectability was assured by its two distinguished Catholic members: Alcalá Zamora, who was Prime Minister, and Miguel Maura (son of Antonio Maura, Spain's most respected conservative politician) who held the key post of Minister of the Interior. Its main objective was to reduce some of the commanding heights of the old Spain, in particular the Church and the Army, so as to lessen the danger to the new liberalism.

A government which was an alliance of such differing interests might well have been forgiven for moving slowly and cautiously in order to root the infant Republic firmly in Spain's unpredictable political loyalties. However, no such reasonable or tactical spirit guided the government in its dealing with the Church, an institution so patently an embodiment of the old Spain but still for many Spaniards the source of spiritual comfort and solace. According to Article 3 of the constitution Church and State were to be separate, and this proposition was neither unjust nor fiercely divisive, as was shown by the vote in the Cortes of 278 in favour to 41 against. The constitution's drafters, the Juridical Commission, had also recommended special provisions for the Church, recognising its place in Spanish life, allowing it to maintain its own schools, and even to give religious instruction in the state schools. Such moderation was unpopular with the more militant anti-clericals in the Cortes, not only because of the Church's entrenched position in the old order, but also because of the recent bitter attacks upon the infant Republic by the leader of the Catholic Church in Spain, Cardinal Segura, Archbishop of Toledo. As a result, when the Cortes debated Article 26, which embodied these provisions, the decision was taken to amend them. Now it was stipulated that within two years the state's payment to the clergy was to end and the religious orders who controlled many of the primary and secondary schools of Spain – amongst them some of Spain's best schools and teachers – were to be banned from teaching. As Gerald Brenan [2] points out, the religious clauses of the constitution threw away an opportunity to build republican support in the lower ranks of the Church. Instead the parish priest saw the new government, already damned as godless by his Cardinal-Primate, cutting off his income and forcing him into even closer dependence on the wealthy. When Article 26 finally went through the Cortes, voting had slumped to 178 in favour to 59 against, with nearly half the Cortes abstaining. Both Maura and Alcalá Zamora resigned over this clause – although Alcalá Zamora returned as President. The new Prime Minister was Manuel Azaña, President of Madrid's most famous literary and political club, the *Ateneo*, an able and honest man, but militantly anti-clerical. Azaña, as Minister for War, had already begun the task of dismantling that other major citadel of Spanish traditionalism, the Spanish Army [32; 14].

In the past, the Army had swept aside governments and re-made constitutions [3]. That such a danger still remained in the Spain of the Republic was quite clear and the Army reforms of the new government were directed to removing, or at least reducing, this threat. What Azaña sought to do was to make the size of the Army more in keeping with the needs of a country which was unlikely ever again to be involved in another major war. The Army was top-heavy (often literally so, with generals so overweight that they could not easily mount a horse), with 22,000 officers, of whom over 500 were generals, to 165,000 men. Azaña's reforms were comprehensive. To all generals and most other officers, he offered retirement on full pay – an offer which half the officer corps took advantage of; he closed the élite military academy at Saragossa (where Franco was in charge); and in order to democratise the Army he reserved places for NCOs in military academies. Azaña's main concern was with modernisation of the structure rather than the technology of the Army, and his reforms were carried through without consultation with his senior officers. These reforms were financially generous, even expensive, for any saving could take place only as retired officers were removed by death; but the effect of this pruning of the senior ranks was to conserve an officer corps in which the hard-core professionals, the *africanistas*, were dominant, and it left them bruised and resentful of a policy which, in their view, had 'placed party ideals above national ideals' [15]. One reform brought Spain into line with most other European countries: the introduction of universal conscription. Liability included one year in active service, but a complicated exemption system was built in which required, for instance, only four weeks' service from those with certain educational qualifications. Another proviso allowed a conscript to buy himself out after six months' service, which had the effect of requiring more military service from the poor than from the rich [15].

In the conservative interpretation of her history, Spain's greatness had depended not only on the Catholic Church but on the maintenance of unity, a unity forged by Castile and stemming from Castile, and from which both empire and Spain's eternal values had evolved. This vision of Spain's past which had been recently revived by Primo de Rivera – and was to be blown into fresh life by General Franco – was no longer without challenge from the other 'nations' in the Peninsula. In the liberal interpretation, Spain's greatness lay in her pre-imperial history when her political life was based upon *fueros** – ancient forms and constitutions – with freedom as the overriding characteristic of an essentially decentralised society. In the 1930s Liberal Spain was committed to reviving within twentieth-century political terms the image of partnership which this view implied. Furthermore, the Republic was in the Catalans' debt for their help in forcing Alfonso XIII into exile. To honour this obligation necessitated a change in the constitution to fulfil the promise of Catalan autonomy made in the Pact of San Sebastian

(1930), that coalition of Socialists, Liberals and Catalans which established the Republic. To balance the needs of Catalans and Spain was not easy, however, when the Catalan nationalist leader, Colonel Macià, talked of a Catalan Republic within an Iberian federation. The compromise which emerged as the Catalan Statute bitterly offended those who, like the editor of the newspaper *ABC*, saw in it 'the dismemberment of the Country' [42 *p. 90*], for it could be seized on as a precedent by other regionalist groups and lead eventually to a federal Spain. The Statute gave Catalans their own Parliament, and granted equality to Castilian and Catalan as 'national' languages, with a dual control of schools. The 'devolved' government had no sovereignty assigned to it but a sheaf of powers and functions, of which perhaps the most important was local control of public order, at least preserving Catalans from the potential harassment of a police force made up of Southern villagers without any knowledge of the region.

Within its first week, the Republic committed itself to agrarian reform. 'The Government,' so ran its proclamation, 'conscious of the conditions in which the immense mass of peasants live, the neglect of the rural economy and the incongruence of rural rights and present legislation, adopts as a norm of policy the recognition that agrarian legislation should correspond to the social function of land' [9 *p. 166*]. These were bold words in a country with such diverse agrarian problems: lack of water, poor soil, an archaic system of leases, *latifundios* in Andalusia, and the pocket-handkerchief holdings, the *minifundios** in Galicia. A start had been made on irrigation schemes by Primo de Rivera and the Republic took over some of these, employing Spain's greatest expert, Lorenzo Pardo. To deal with the *latifundios* and the problem of the archaic leases, in Castile a very grave problem, an agrarian revolution was needed. By the quality and extent of its reforms in the countryside, the Republic would be judged.

As Minister of Labour, Largo Caballero – who, as a Socialist, had the benefit of working within a party with a clear agrarian programme – issued a series of decrees affecting tenants and labourers. Tenants were to be protected from eviction, while labourers who came together in collectives were promised preferential treatment in the granting of leases – a commitment which had the backing of Socialists and those Catholics concerned with social policy. Day labourers were given a guaranteed eight-hour day – equivalent to a rise in wages – and arbitration boards, developed by Primo in industry, were introduced into the countryside to provide a means of collective bargaining under state supervision. Two other policies were more provocative to landlord interests. By the decree '*términos municipales*' farmers and landlords were prohibited from bringing in migrant labour until the local labour supply was used up, a policy which bore particularly heavily upon migrant workers such as the Galicians. By the decree '*laboreo forzoso*' landowners were forbidden to allow land, which traditionally had been farmed to go out of cultivation; this measure was designed to restrain those landowners who might be tempted to reduce their need for labour by such means. The decree carried the explicit threat that wayward landowners would have any uncultivated land confiscated and handed over to collectives of local workers.

Malefakis sees these decrees as 'a revolution without precedent in Spanish rural life' and observes that 'for the first time the balance of legal rights swung away from the landowners to the rural proletariat' [*9 p. 170*]. Certainly, both decrees were of direct benefit to the rural poor; the first enabled labourers to take a hard line about wages and the second was often invoked by local unions to take over unused land.

To assume, however, that either went any way towards solving the problem of rural poverty is to misjudge the tragic extent of that disease endemic in the Spanish countryside. Unemployment, seasonal in such areas of monoculture as Jaén, a major olive-growing area, and rural indebtedness entrenched in Extremadura and Castile, were problems almost beyond a government whose income depended upon such a narrow tax base.

To deal urgently with what was seen as Spain's most pressing social problem, a Technical Commission was established, chaired by Felipe Sánchez Román, and by late July 1931 it had submitted its report, with a simple, expedient, economical and effective proposal for dealing with the problems of Southern Spain. This proposal was based upon two clear assumptions: that the most pressing need was localised in Southern Spain and that any reform had to cost very little, as the Spanish state had insufficient funds to pay for expropriation of land. Consequently, the Commission restricted its proposals to the South and suggestions that there should be a 'temporary occupation' of estates where the landholding exceeded a certain size. Such 'temporary occupations' would be unspecific in length, so that for all practical purposes the tenants (so recognised because they would be called on to pay a small rent) would become owners. The new tenancies could be individual or they could be based upon 'Peasant Communities', with the right to decide by vote whether within that framework they wished to farm individually or collectively. The Technical Commission proposed that this reform should cover 60,000–75,000 families a year, and it gave itself the long-term objective of completing the process within a period of 12 or 15 years.

Such an effective yet revolutionary reform pleased no one. The landowners were understandably hostile; the Radicals dubbed it 'absurd'; and the Socialists were fearful that a new and reactionary government could easily reverse it. The Socialists demanded a firmer legal framework for any agrarian reform, and their insistence led to a measure which, while legally sound, was not immediately more effective and proved, in the long term, much easier to suspend.

This measure, the Agrarian Reform Bill, which finally went through the Cortes in 1932, was universal in application and provided compensation to landowners for any of their land which was confiscated. The original aim of settling up to 75,000 families a year was quietly dropped, and the bill became discriminatory and punitive – and therefore fundamentally divisive – as a result of amendments made by the Azaña government after the Sanjurjo rising in 1932. In the Cortes, Azaña initially took the view that the nobles were collectively responsible for the rebellion and should therefore all lose part of their land. This proposal, which would have affected some 2,000 families, was whittled down in the course of debate and ultimately applied only to the upper nobility, 262 families of whom only two, in fact, had been associated with Sanjurjo's rising.

Although revolutionary in its implications, with an Institute of Agrarian Reform to oversee its operations, the Agrarian Reform Law brought little change to the countryside before Azaña's ministry was replaced in 1933 by a right-wing government anxious to abandon the whole policy of land transfer. In the end, fewer than 7,000 families benefited and no more than 45,000 hectares were redistributed. If, as the Provisional Government had foreseen, the rural problem was *the* problem of contemporary Spain, the new Republic had done very little to solve it.

THE SANJURJADA, 1932

The euphoric mood in which the Republic had been launched, charted in detail by Shlomo Ben-Ami [26], did not outlast its first year. A disillusioned Ortega was, by then, calling for the formation of a 'party of national breadth' and castigating the new Republic as

'sad and sour' [42 *p. 84*]. So rapid a turnabout from so eminent a
Republican lent support to a Catholic right wing understandably
incensed by the new laws against the Church. Catholic intellectuals
had devised, in the doctrine of 'accidentalism', a means to deal with
just such a problem as now faced them: a hostile exercise of the
state power. Accidentalism implied that the form of the state (a
Republic) was unimportant: what was important was to secure the
rights of the Church within it. The Catholic leader, Ángel Herrera,
defined his position as 'fighting to improve the legislation within the
established constitution' [42 *p. 75*].

What was far more dangerous was the growth of disaffection in
the Army. The problem of public order, how it was to be defined
and how maintained, was the root cause of Army hostility. The
official guardian of public order was the Civil Guard, an armed
force, patrolling always in twos, and originally established to stamp
out rural banditry. Traditionally, this was a sub-military force, and
behaved often with the insensitivity of an occupying army. Peasant
and working-class hatred of the Civil Guard was endemic and the
Republic changed nothing, except to set up a new security force, the
Assault Guards – a gesture which could be seen as conciliatory. The
early days of the Republic were marred by a series of clashes
between the populace and the Civil Guard, beginning in 1931 with
an incident in Castilblanco, in Extremadura, when several Guards
were killed. General Sanjurjo, its Director, declared that 'the Guard
would not tolerate cowardly attacks upon itself in the future' and
three days later two peasants in the province of Badajoz were shot
by the Guards; these deaths were followed quickly by six others in
widely differing parts of Spain. This grisly week of revenge
culminated with the death in Arnedo, in Logroño, of seven workers
demonstrating outside the town hall. Faced by a press outcry, Azaña
dismissed Sanjurjo – even though he had claims to be regarded as a
founding father of the Republic, since he had refused to support the
monarchy with his armed forces in the critical period following the
municipal elections.

To Sanjurjo, who in this was typical of Army leaders, as to many
rural landowners, public order rested ultimately upon the salutary
use of armed force, the assumption that the social hierarchy, with its
starving or near-starving base, must depend upon the willingness to
crack a few skulls. His dismissal, then, could be read, by him as by
others, as evidence of a pusillanimous government's willingness to
permit rural anarchy. Already different groups were planning to
overthrow Azaña, groups ranging from monarchist politicians and

monarchist generals to right-wing Republicans such as Melquiades Álvarez and *africanistas* like General Goded. To these groups General Sanjurjo naturally gravitated, beginning a grand tour of Spain, concentrating on the garrison towns, and whipping up support for his own plan, which centred round the capture of Azaña. His scheme was not ostensibly monarchist, to replace republic by monarchy, but merely a *pronunciamiento* with the limited aim of setting up a right-wing government.

On the day appointed (10 August 1932) the conspirators in Madrid hardly stirred, although in Seville and in Jérez the *sanjurjada** was successful. Faced, however, with a largely unresponsive Spain, the General abandoned his plans, gave himself up, and was sentenced to death – though this was subsequently commuted to life imprisonment. In 1934 the new right-wing government pardoned the General, together with the other conspirators, and he retired to Portugal. There he remained until, in 1936, he left once more for Spain to head the new and successful rising. He never arrived, however, for his overloaded plane crashed on take-off.

Although the 1932 Rising recruited so little support – estimated by Stanley Payne as only 5 per cent of the Spanish officer corps [15] – it was a grim reminder that within the Army there still persisted the nineteenth-century conviction that it reflected the national will more accurately than the politicians and an elected Cortes.

THE INSURRECTION OF 1934

Disenchantment with the Republic had affected groups other than high-ranking Army officers. On the right, *Acción Nacional*, renamed *Acción Popular* in 1932, burgeoned into CEDA, a grouping of most of the parliamentary, legalist Right, reflecting the views of landholders, the Catholic middle class, and all those who saw the danger to Spain as the threat from the Left, and the reform of the Church–State laws as the immediate need. The rhetoric of its leader, Gil Robles, and the rank-and-file militancy, particularly from its youth movement, JAP,* pushed CEDA publicly more and more towards the concept of a corporate state and a total revision of the new democratic structure of the Republic. To committed Republicans, and particularly to the Left, Gil Robles represented the threat of Spanish fascism, and with the contemporary evidence of Hitler's legal seizure of power before their eyes, they feared that CEDA's entry into government would be the beginning of a fascist take-over. Nothing in Gil Robles's style of leadership suggested a firm commitment to Republican institutions. In the 1933 electoral campaign, for instance, he called for 'a totalitarian policy' and asserted that 'Democracy is not an end but a means to the conquest of the new state . . . when the time comes, either parliament submits or we will eliminate it' [36 *p. 48*].

Attachment to the Republic, to a liberal parliamentary regime, was perhaps restricted by 1933 to middle-class liberals such as Azaña or Casares Quiroga, who saw Spain's problems in constitutional or political terms, to be solved by the Army reforms and Church–State legislation. They did not regard the fiscal, social and economic reforms necessary to transform Spain, to reduce the blatant inequalities between Spaniards, and to raise the standard of life of the rural and urban poor, as the fundamental means by which the Republic could be defended. In retrospect it might be argued that the maintenance of the Republic really required an extension of its moral frontiers, in order to take in those Spaniards for whom 1931 had made only a marginal difference, and thereby obtain the active co-operation, instead of merely the passive obedience, of Spain's labouring poor.

The extent to which the Republic had failed to win over the politically active in the working class was shown not only in the continuing strikes and disturbances but also in the continuing debate upon tactics which ran through the working-class movement. Under Primo de Rivera the CNT, increasingly moderate and trade-union-oriented in leadership, had been persecuted and suppressed and its leaders had gone underground or into exile [11]. Repression whetted anarchist militancy and this new mood gave rise to the FAI*, founded in 1927 at Valencia by Spanish and Portuguese anarchists. The FAI, the Iberian Federation of Anarchists, remained profoundly Spanish rather than Iberian and was based upon the 'affinity group', a 'family' of a dozen or so members. By the eve of the Civil War its total membership was probably under 40,000, but from its ranks sprang men like Durruti and Abad de Santillán, together with anarchist *incontrolados** who resisted all control and initiated their own terrorist policies. The FAI was clandestine, conspiratorial and committed to violent revolution and the use of terror. When the CNT re-emerged under the Republic, leading syndicalists such as Ángel Pestaña proclaimed their opposition to the cult of violence in a famous manifesto, signed by thirty members (the *Treintistas*) which precipitated a major debate on tactics [99].

Within Spanish socialism, the PSOE and the UGT showed signs of increasing alienation from the 'bourgeois' Republic. There was disagreement on the tactical wisdom of initial participation in the coalition, with Prieto and Largo Caballero defending in different degree the reformist path, while the PSOE's most distinguished theoretician, Julián Besteiro, argued that such participation might make a fascist seizure of power easier to achieve [9; 36]. The Socialists' decision to withdraw from an electoral pact with the Republicans meant competition between former allies for parliamentary seats and helped to produce in the November 1933 elections a Centre-Right Cortes, with Socialist numbers falling from 120 to 58, and CEDA emerging as the numerically strongest group with 114 seats, followed by the Lerroux Radicals with 104. Despite the strength in the Cortes of the CEDA group, the President, Alcalá Zamora, declined to invite Gil Robles to form a government and chose instead Lerroux and his 'historic' Republicans.

During 1934 first Lerroux and then his successor, Samper, aroused working-class and liberal hostility by ignoring much of the reform legislation that the Azaña government had passed. Agrarian reform almost ceased; clerical control of education reappeared as Church schools continued to function and the school building programme was sharply reduced. Even the decision to end state payments to the Catholic clergy was reversed. The Catalans, sensitive to Madrid's change of direction, had their own grievances. The Catalan Parliament, the *Generalitat*, had enacted a law allowing *rabassaires* (tenants of vineyards) the right to purchase land which they had cultivated for fifteen years. This was a complex issue, which in Catalonia divided landlords from tenants, and Madrid vetoed the law – a rejection seen by militant Catalans as an attack upon Catalan autonomy and by the left as further evidence of Madrid's hostility to agrarian reform. A complicating factor was the political difference between Catalonia's Left-inclined government, headed by Luis Companys, and the Centre-Right government in Madrid.

When on 1 October the Cortes reassembled after the summer recess, Prime Minister Samper, the President and Spain were faced by a major political crisis, brought about when Gil Robles withdrew CEDA's parliamentary support from the government. The President had few options, for no government could survive without CEDA. He would therefore have to call a general election unless he offered power to CEDA. Alcalá Zamora, however, shared Left and Left-Republican suspicions of Gil Robles's political intentions and was unwilling to ask him to head a government. Instead he compromised, by taking the constitutionally correct course of inviting the Radical, Lerroux, to form a new coalition government, with three ministries reserved for CEDA, thus avoiding a CEDA government which would be offensive to liberals and socialists, yet allowing CEDA a share in that political power which by virtue of its numbers it had a right to expect [37].

The reactions of liberal Republicans and Socialists showed little understanding of the constitutional niceties of the situation. Republicans such as Azaña, Martínez Barrio and Miguel Maura promptly accused the President of handing the Republic over to its enemies. The Socialists voted for a general strike, using the strike weapon for political purposes as they had unsuccessfully tried to do in the republican plot of 1930 [3]. In Barcelona, pushed by Catalan nationalists, Companys announced that Catalonia would henceforth be a separate state 'within the federal Spanish Republic'. This assertion of independence was short-lived, however, and ended without serious bloodshed.

The general strike was a fiasco and there was no further resistance to the new government except in the Asturias. There, in the mining villages around Oviedo, the united Left took decisive action. On the night of 4 October the miners of Mieres rose in revolt and forced the surrender of Civil Guards and Assault Guards. Within two days the Asturian miners had captured the greater part of the provincial capital of Oviedo. Armed mainly with the dynamite used in mining operations, the miners seized two arms factories and established political and military control. The moderates held in check those who wanted to carry out private or class revenge [31].

The War Minister, Diego Hidalgo, acting on the advice of General Franco and General Goded, sent in, not the Spanish conscripts, but the Foreign Legion and the Moorish troops, the *Regulares*. By 18 October the whole region had been recaptured, with Mieres the last town to fall. The assault against the Asturian villages had been marked by great barbarity, and sometimes in captured villages anyone found hiding was shot [31] [*Doc.1*]. The suppression of the revolt was followed by wholesale arrests, and suspects were tortured, under the orders of a certain Major Doval of the Civil Guard. As a consequence of the October events, the government held around 40,000 prisoners, and dealt with Catalonia by suspending the autonomy statute. It then called for the death sentence not only on leaders but also on others – like Teodomiro Menéndez, a Socialist deputy in Oviedo – who had taken no part in the rising, or like González Peña, a moderate UGT organiser who had helped to control the more militant revolutionaries. Prime

Minister Lerroux was under strong pressure from Gil Robles and CEDA to carry out the death sentences, but in the end he commuted them.

The 1934 events left the Socialists in complete disarray. Prieto was in voluntary exile, and Largo Caballero, with many other prominent socialists, was in prison. The initiative now lay with the Right to try to win over working-class Spain by a generous and humane policy. 'After the revolution of 1934 and the manner in which it had been quelled', writes Hugh Thomas, 'it would have required a super-human effort to avoid the culminating disaster of civil war . . . but no such effort was forthcoming' [85 *p. 145*].

From the viewpoint of the Spanish Left, the Asturian Rising was an attempt to prevent the imposition of an authoritarian regime on Spain, with Spanish workers refusing to follow the example of passive acceptance set by their German socialist friends when faced by Hitler. In another sense, the insurrection could more properly be seen not as an attempt at revolution, but as a blood sacrifice, a demonstration of working-class determination to take up arms in the defence of the Republic, and a warning to the extreme Right of the dangers implicit in any authoritarian coup. For the constitutionalist Right, 1934 provided ominous evidence that socialists as well as anarchists were prepared to abandon constitutional forms. However, in undermining middle-class belief in the political reliability of the Left, the events of 1934 must be judged disastrous. Gerald Brenan, on the other hand, argues that the 'stupidity of the Right' transformed the rebellion into 'an enormous moral and political success' [2 *p. 292*]. The price for Spain was tragically high, for 1934 lent credibility to the stories of left-wing conspiracy by which the Army 'justified' the 1936 Military Rising. After the Asturian Insurrection the undermining of the Republic was already well under way. Both 1932 and 1934 had left the Republic balanced upon an ever-narrowing base.

POLITICS AND PARTIES ON THE EVE OF THE CIVIL WAR

In the Spain of the mid-1930s, political parties were distinguished from each other in many different ways. One major dividing line was commitment to the Republic itself. On the Right were monarchists-Carlists, Alfonsists, even sections of CEDA which were bitterly hostile to the Republic and impatient for a return to a more traditional Spain. A second litmus test was commitment to the constitutional forms created by the 1931 Revolution. Both on the Right and Left, parties existed which rejected the democratic

framework of the state – the Carlists, the Alfonsists, the Falange,*
and on the Left, the CNT, the PCE,* and POUM* in Catalonia. A
deep-seated localism also played its part, reflected in the regionalist
parties which ran from the well-established parties in Catalonia and
the Basque Provinces to the smaller but still influential groups in
Galicia and Valencia. Two other factors helped decide political
attitudes: one was social class, and the other religious belief – or
lack of it. The Right drew its support from the aristocracy and from
the great landowners, from the wealthy bankers like Juan March,
from the Catholic Church and from Catholic peasant farmers. Its
leaders were ambitious Catholic politicians like Gil Robles (who had
married the daughter of one of Spain's richest aristocrats), thought
devious even by his own party, or Calvo Sotelo, in exile after 1931
for his responsibility for the *dictadura*, but returning on the tide of
right-wing electoral victory in 1933 and campaigning openly for the
destruction of the Republic. On the Left, the PSOE at the local level
was based on the UGT and the urban working class, but in the
Cortes its deputies were mainly from the intellectual (and often
anti-clerical) middle class, men such as Julián Besteiro or Fernando
de los Rios, with the working-class Largo Caballero and Indalecio
Prieto the exception. The Centre ground was occupied by the
Radicals and the Left Republicans. The Radicals, led by Alejandro
Lerroux, a notoriously corrupt politician, were essentially
anti-clerical but without much intellectual ballast. On the other
hand, Azaña's Left Republicans, doctrinaire Liberals and
anti-clericals, were the initial driving force behind the Second
Republic's reforms. Again, they were essentially middle class,
fundamentally the university-educated intelligentsia. The Spanish
Cortes in 1936 could well be seen as representative of articulate
Spain, with the Republican parties led by deputies steeped in
nineteenth century Liberal ideas, and the Right, apart from the
Falange, nostalgically looking back to the traditional hierarchical
Spain of the monarchy.

Of the right-wing 'catastrophist' parties (a designation intended to
publicise their shared conviction that only counter-revolution could
overturn the despised Republic) two were monarchist, the Carlists
and the Alfonsists, albeit with differing royal candidates and
differing ideologies. The Carlists, in 1931 renamed the Traditional
Communion, were by far the senior of the two (occasional)
partners. Unlike the Alfonsists, they had a historical constituency, in
Navarre, and a paramilitary force, the *requetés*.* Furthermore, the
Carlists had elected five deputies to the 1931 Cortes, rising in 1936

to eight. Their power base was further extended when Fal Conde, a Seville lawyer, began to proselytise amongst the Catholic youth in the major cities of Andalusia, and local branches were set up in Córdoba, Granada and Jérez, with funds coming from the sherry dynasties such as Domecq and Gonzalez. Such growth may well have been affected by the virtual collapse of the traditional right-wing parties after Alfonso's flight, but as Martin Blinkhorn [49] points out, this new shoot differed profoundly from the main body in the North, not only because it developed in hitherto virgin territory but because its leadership was so relatively youthful. The main body of monarchist opinion looked to the return of Alfonso XIII, to the restoration of an authoritarian regime. Some Alfonsist monarchists took refuge in CEDA, ostensibly committed to legalism. Others, led by Antonio Goicoechea, founded a separate political party, *Renovación Española*, committed to counter-revolution. When Calvo Sotelo took over its leadership, he changed its name to *Bloque Nacional*,* specifically intended as a party designed to work for the creation of a comprehensive right-wing movement, bringing together CEDA, the Carlists and the Falangists. The *Bloque* campaigned for a strong state capable of imposing both order and social justice. The original aim of restoring Alfonso now gave way to a new emphasis on authoritarianism. The Spain of the future would be strike-free, starvation-wages would disappear, together with 'anarchic liberty'. This political initiative won no support from CEDA, or for that matter from the country at large. In the elections of 1936 Calvo Sotelo won only 11 seats. This clear evidence of failure to create a national movement did not deter Calvo Sotelo in Parliament from speaking as if he were the voice of the nation. He warned of the imminent danger of communism. He spoke of the need for an 'integrated state', which, as he said, if called 'fascist', 'I proudly call myself fascist'. Outside Parliament, he was in busy contact either directly or through an intermediary with the plotters in the Army and in the Falange. In Paul Preston's view [78] Calvo's most significant contribution to the Rising was his behaviour in Parliament, with inflammatory speeches which drove a wedge between moderates on both sides, and which provoked parliamentary behaviour which brought Parliament into disrepute.

The Falange alone of the 'catastrophist' parties had anything approaching a social programme, although paradoxically its main support came from university students, who, in the 1930s, were very much a privileged class. Since its founding in 1933, the Falange Española had been led by José Antonio Primo de Rivera, the son of the dictator, a loyal son dedicated to clearing his father's memory and name. From the beginning, the movement had the benefit of the poetic, if cloudy, rhetoric of which José Antonio was a master. He promised an end to political parties, a rejection of outworn nineteenth-century liberalism and a kind of social justice [46]. Within a year the Falange was expanded by the inclusion of a national syndicalist group, the *Juntas de Ofensiva Nacional-Sindicalista* (JONS),* led by a Madrid University philosophy graduate Ramiro Ledesma, and from this group the Falange was to take not only its symbol, the yoked arrows of the Catholic Kings, but many of its most successful slogans. Ledesma's national syndicalism was to distinguish Falangism from other European fascist movements and to give it some right to see itself as both radical and peculiarly Spanish, in that it shared with the native anarcho-syndicalists a commitment to reshaping industry through labour syndicates which would 'organise Spanish society along corporative lines, by means of a system of vertical unions representing the various branches of production' [22 *p. 134*] [*Doc. 4*].

In the original Twenty-Six Point Programme of the Falange, published in 1934, José Antonio roundly condemned the capitalist system, 'which disregards the needs of the people, dehumanizes private property and transforms the workers into shapeless masses prone to misery and despair' [22 *p. 134*] [*Doc. 4*]. Point 15 proclaimed that 'All Spanish citizens are entitled to employment' and promised a social security system in which 'the public institutions will provide for the maintenance of those who are involuntarily out of work'. The programme also addressed itself to what was widely accepted as *the* Spanish social problem, that of rural despair, symbolised by the Andalusian labourer hired by the day and unemployed for much of the year. Point 19 promised to reorganise agriculture 'by redistributing all the arable land so as to promote family holdings' and 'by rescuing the masses of people, who are exhausting themselves scratching on barren soil, from their present poverty and transferring them to new holdings of arable land' [22 *p. 136*].

At the outbreak of the Asturian insurrection, the local Falangist militia had offered support to the military and taken part in the suppression of the workers in Gijon and Oviedo. Five members were lost in action. As the single Falangist member in the Cortes, José Antonio proffered his own analysis of its causes, contrasting the 'mystical sense of rebellion' which inspired the miners with the total absence of any mystical fervour on the government's side. In effect, he was proposing the Falange as the only force which could supply that necessary mystical ardour to offset the sterility of the established parties.

In 1934, Calvo Sotelo, recently returned from exile, and enthused by ideas culled from French and Portuguese fascism, suggested that his *Renovación Española*, the Alfonsist party, should join forces with José Antonio. This looked like a marriage made in heaven, combining the great wealth of the Andalusian landowners with the charismatic charm of the son of Primo de Rivera, still seen nostalgically as presiding over Spain's golden age. The *Jefe Nacional**, however, not only disliked Calvo but would not contemplate any union with a party whose vision of the future consisted entirely of a return to the past.

His contempt for liberalism was similarly deep-rooted. In a speech in Vallodolid in 1935, José Antonio spelt out its fundamental contradictions. 'Liberalism', he declared, 'told men that they could do as they liked, but failed to provide men with an economic order which would guarantee such freedom' [22 *p. 146*]. To the Spanish poor the classical liberal freedoms were meaningless. Indeed, economic liberalism, he argued, was unsuited to a country like Spain which had never experienced the heroic age of capitalism, and had failed to develop in the traditional Western European manner. 'In Spain', as he observed, 'big business resorted to state aid from the outset' [22 *p. 170*].

Social radicalism such as this repelled the Spanish Right and yet Falangism was unable to win support from a working class traditionally committed to socialism or anarchism. Its main appeal was to students and to tiny minorities, dissatisfied with the sterility of the Catholic and conservative parties of Spain, who could not find a political home in the left-wing parties. To these groups Falangism, more than any other right-wing party, seemed to offer a possible alternative, a vision of a revived and powerful Spain, but a Spain with more concern for social justice.

His sympathy for the social concerns of the Spanish Left induced José Antonio to try to win over members of the CNT and PSOE. Indalecio Prieto he greatly admired, so much so that he suggested that the Falangists and *prietistas** should unite, with Prieto leading a united Socialist Falange. Such a party, he thought, might draw in the anti-Marxist members of the CNT. With a mere 5,000 members, the Falange could bring little to such a match and no progress was made on this imaginative, but politically unrealistic, proposal.

In the years before the outbreak of the Civil War, Falangists and left-wing extremists fought and killed each other in the streets. To stem the growing violence, the Azaña government in March 1936 arrested José Antonio and banned the Falange. It was, therefore, from his prison in Madrid, and later in Alicante, that José Antonio, as its *Jefe Nacional*, led his now illegal movement. The Falangist leader's attitude to the military conspiracy was one of profound suspicion. Initially, he specifically forbade his supporters to take part in any conspiracy against the Popular Front government. His hostility may have arisen from an unsatisfactory meeting with Franco just before the February elections, when José Antonio was insisting on the need for immediate military action to set up a national government. Franco was at his most evasive. The after-effects of this meeting may be seen again in José Antonio's manoeuvres to prevent Franco standing as candidate in the re-run by-election in Cuenca in May. For the *Jefe Nacional*, winning this election would give him parliamentary immunity and release from prison. If Franco stood as well, José Antonio's electoral chances would almost certainly be reduced. In the event, although the Falange chief won sufficient votes, he was disqualified on a technicality. Franco never forgot – and possibly never forgave – the Falangist leader's part in this affair. In the months after the Popular Front's victory at the polls, the Falange, claiming that Marxism had now taken over Spain, enjoyed a dramatic expansion in membership, rising from 5,000 to 500,000 within less than six months [62]. Clearly, within the Spanish Right, moderates were abandoning the constitutional parties and making ready for a seizure of power: accidentalism was giving way to catastrophism.

After the murder of Calvo Sotelo in July, José Antonio threatened to send the Alicante Falange into the streets to begin the Rising independently if General Mola, the 'Director' of the military conspiracy, did not take immediate action. The Falangist leader was convinced that the military leaders had no capacity for politics and that the political initiative must be seized by the Falange when the Rising began.

Established in 1933, CEDA, ostensibly, was the face of moderate conservatism, a Christian Democratic party committed publicly to working within the Republican constitution. Its doctrine of 'accidentalism' implied a political willingness to accept the events of 1931. How far, if at all, was this position maintained, only to be abandoned at the outbreak of the Civil War? In interpreting the role and activities of CEDA in the early 1930s, historians differ profoundly. Some, such as Richard A. H. Robinson, see CEDA as fundamentally a constitutional party forced reluctantly into direct action by the antics of the revolutionary Left [42]; for others, such as Paul Preston, CEDA was skilled in hiding its inflexible opposition to the Republic behind a cloak of legality [36]. Certainly, both at the national and local level evidence may be found to support either interpretation.

Within its ranks, Ceda had many moderates prepared to work within the system. However, its normal public stance was far from moderate. The tone of a democratic party is set by its leader, and increasingly Gil Robles came to be seen as controlling a party whose political style and stance seemed overtly fascist. Although Gil Robles himself cannot be accused of plotting to overthrow the government, he ran public meetings which seemed replicas of fascist rallies, with clamorous, emotional calls for the *Jefe*. Addressing one such meeting, individual CEDA deputies railed 'against Jews, heretics, freemasons, liberals and Marxists'. Another deputy, Serrano Súñer, condemned 'degenerate democracy'. Such mass displays of blind obedience to the Leader, such Nazi-style language, appeared ominous and a threat to the Left. Again, the political intentions of CEDA were clearly signalled in their dismantling of the reforms of the 1931–33 Republican-Socialist coalition. In and out of Parliament, in his speeches, Gil Robles seemed to be outlining a Spain of the future in which working-class parties and movements would have no place. In 1934, for instance, in the wake of the Asturian Rising, Gil Robles proposed to Parliament that trade unions should be abolished, and their funds confiscated to pay for the costs of the Rising. However, as no evidence could be found to implicate the trade unions, such a proposal had no basis in law and had to be abandoned. Clearly, although not all *cedistas** shared his vision, Gil Robles saw the corporate state as the ideal model for Spain. However, despite this conviction and its implicit rejection of Spain's democratic republic, he was, until the failure of the Right to win the 1936 elections, essentially a 'legalist'. In his view, the new state framework would be set up by working initially within the democratic system. With CEDA in power, the transformation would then take place, not by *coup d'état* or military rising, but by a parliamentary majority. The model here could be found in the German experience, where Hitler and the Nazi party had come to power by constitutional means.

With the victory of the Popular Front, wealthy backers withdrew support from Gil Robles and turned to Calvo Sotelo. In despair, *cedistas* abandoned legality. At the local level, for instance in

Valencia [33], the youth section of the party were already involved in paramilitary activity as early as 1935, working with the Falangists and Carlists. The local party, always ambivalent in its attitude to the Republic, came to believe that only a national rising could save Spain. At the national level, although he took no personal part in the army plot, Gil Robles was privy to it and transferred CEDA funds to General Mola, the master-mind of the conspiracy. He also instructed individual *cedistas* to put themselves at the disposal of the Army as soon as the Rising began. Thus the Spanish Right gave a political dimension to the military plotters.

The Spanish Socialist Party, the PSOE, the constitutional party of the Left, was still suffering in the early months of 1936 from the after-effects of the 1934 Asturian Rising. Of the 30,000 political prisoners still held after the Rising, many were Socialist Party members, including Largo Caballero, its leader. Prieto, the tactician of the party, had chosen voluntary exile in France rather than suffer imprisonment. Between the two leading Socialists there was a great deal of hostility, based in part on personalities and in part on differing interpretations of the road to socialism. Prieto, a man of great intelligence, who, in his native Bilbao, had risen from newsboy to newspaper proprietor, had the gift of eloquence – he was the best speaker in Parliament – and an ease of manner which won the hearts of the middle classes. Largo, on the other hand, by trade a Madrid plasterer, puritanical and dour, was never a successful parliamentarian, yet had the support and respect of working-class voters. Where they differed, most disastrously for the Socialist Party and most dangerously for Spain, was in tactics. Prieto's approach was gradualist: he considered that a broad-based coalition such as that of 1931–33 would be the most effective means of making Spain a more just society. The mistake, in his view, had been to abandon the Republican-Socialist pact in the 1933 elections, thereby allowing the Right to win, albeit by only a small margin. Largo Caballero, in prison, had re-thought his own position, and in his public statements was assuming a markedly revolutionary stance. His increasing identification of himself as the Spanish Lenin with Azaña playing the role of Kerensky, made a 1917-style bolshevik revolution in Spain seem the pattern of the future. Within the PSOE, theoreticians of the Left such as Luis Araquistain pushed for 'bolshevisation', and were committed to destroying the influence of the reformist wing of the party [49].

The PSOE, like most European socialist parties, was Marxist, but independent of the Third International, the Comintern, which was controlled by the Soviet Union. Its traditional position was similar to that of the German Social Democrats or the British Labour Party: to secure social justice by parliamentary means. However, on his release from prison, Largo Caballero's speeches calling for revolution struck fear into the heart of middle-class Spain, and led increasingly to the widespread conviction that revolution was imminent, with Spain threatened by communism. That no genuine threat existed was evident in that the PSOE, unlike the Carlists or Falangists, had no para-military force. Again, Largo Caballero made one profoundly unwise tactical mistake in failing to prevent the union of the youth section of the party, the FJS, with the youth section of the PCE, thereby allowing the FJS to fall under the control of the Comintern. His failure to oppose this could be interpreted as fulfilling the need for proletarian unity which Largo Caballero saw as a prime necessity for a working-class party. However, this fusion of the two youth movements meant in part an abandonment of the Spanish Socialists' hitherto total independence of Moscow [49].

How then, with such a theoretical base, did Largo Caballero join with the Republican parties in the Popular Front? Or to stand the question on its head: how did a staunchly constitutional party such as Azaña's Left Republicans form an electoral pact with Largo Caballero's ostensibly revolutionary Socialists? To state the question in this way implies a conviction on Azaña's part that the Socialist leader's threats of revolution were no more than political posturing, in themselves a kind of political theatre, at the least unwise, if not downright dangerous, in the volatile political climate of 1936.

The centre ground in Spanish politics, held by the Republican parties, had by 1936 become more clearly defined. There were several small parties, but the two with strong roots in the 1931 Republic were the Radicals, led by Alejandro Lerroux, and the Left Republicans of Manuel Azaña. The Radicals, hostile to the Socialists, had shared power with CEDA despite the strident anti-clericalism of its leader. The son of a sergeant major, Lerroux had emerged from Barcelona as founder of the Radical Party and had rapidly become very rich, on the way acquiring a well-deserved reputation for corruption.

At the other end of the moral spectrum was Azaña, one of the 30,000 Spaniards imprisoned after the 1934 Rising, but subsequently acquitted for lack of evidence. He was a man of austere habits, scholarly, with great gifts as a leader and initiator of policy. The architect of the Republic from 1931–33, eloquent and high-minded, he was to become the symbol of the Republic's resistance to Francoism after 1936. Picturesquely ugly, and consequently solitary, he led a life of dedication to scholarship and to politics. Hostile to Church and Army, the twin pillars of the Right, to his supporters he represented the best in the Spanish character. Broué and Témime sum up his policy as directed to giving 'priority to a programme of reforms capable of winning over enough workers to check the revolutionary movement' [*51 p. 48*]. Azaña's party, the Left Republicans, was the larger of the two major Republican parties. The other was led by a freemason, Diego Martinez Barrio, a man of great personal integrity, who had, with his supporters, left the discredited Radical Party to form the Republican Union.

On the far Left, a version of 'catastrophism' thrived in the social and political millenarianism of the CNT. If one looked for a parallel to Carlism, with its devoted attachment to a lost cause, anarcho-syndicalism would be the obvious choice. Like Carlism, anarcho-syndicalism in the Europe of the 1930s was almost entirely native to Spain. Rural Navarre, a land of independent wealthy farmers, and staunchly Catholic, supported Carlism: the neighbouring province of Aragon, dominated by a network of landowning families with a stranglehold on village and local government, had become, by the 1930s, a major anarchist stronghold.

The libertarian movement in Aragon reached back to the 1870s, taking root first in the capital, Saragossa, and other provincial towns like Huesca and Teruel, and then spreading out into the nearby villages. Its fortunes differed with the level of repression deployed by the central and local government. With the end of the *dictadura*, the CNT was able to establish branches throughout most of Aragon. Although the CNT there took no part in the events of October 1934, nevertheless it suffered equally from the repression of the years 1934–35.

With the fall of the Radical–CEDA government, the subsequent caretaker government of Portela Valladares permitted the re-establishment in 1936 of active trade unionism, and in Aragon once more the anarchist movement sprang back into new life. At its regional congress in April, the Aragonese CNT disregarded the usual minutiae of branch meetings and looked to the future with an agenda dominated by land reform, centring on the creation of agrarian collectives. The strength of the CNT in Aragon may be judged by the number of organised branches recorded at the CNT national congress held in Zaragoza in May. In all, there were 278 unions represented from Aragon, compared with less than 200 for

Catalonia and no more than 312 from the heartland of rural anarchism, Andalusia and Extremadura. Fittingly, it was in Aragon that the anarchist dream of giving land to its workers was fulfilled in the months after the outbreak of the Civil War. In the South, Franco's airborne invasion and his *Reconquista* made such an agrarian experiment impossible.

If Aragon was a major centre of rural millenarian anarchism, semi-industrialised Catalonia, on the other hand, was a flourishing centre of CNT trade-union activity of a more traditional kind. There were still unco-ordinated strikes and armed risings committed to achieving that new society which anarchists held to be inevitable, yet there was also a growing emphasis on the syndicalist aspect, on trade unionism as a means of improving working conditions. In the 1936 elections the Barcelona CNT showed a marked shift from its traditional abstentionism and went to the polls to support the electoral promise of an amnesty for political prisoners, which the Popular Front had promised.

None of the other left-wing parties had the mass support of either the CNT or the PSOE. The Spanish Communist Party had no more than 30,000 members in 1936 and only one nationally known leader, Dolores Ibarruri Gomez, La Pasionaria, a powerful orator, who, after the 1934 Rising, had been sentenced to fifteen years' imprisonment. In Catalonia, when the Civil War began, the residual Communist Party there merged with other left-wing groups to become the PSUC*. The POUM, immortalised by George Orwell, was even smaller. In 1936, it had at most 3,000 supporters, mainly in Catalonia. It had been formed in 1934 from a fragment of Spanish communism. Denounced by Trotsky, its political enemies still persisted in labelling it Trotskyist. POUM saw itself as the sole inheritor of the ideals of Lenin and of communism, the one true revolutionary party, opposed to Stalinist communism and to parliamentary socialism alike.

THE POPULAR FRONT

In the run-up to the February elections, the Left Republicans, Spain's quintessential Liberal Party, found themselves moving in the same direction as the Socialist politician, Indalecio Prieto. The Republican leader, Manuel Azaña, was touring Spain, calling for a new Centre-Left pact, and finding everywhere an enthusiastic response. At the same time he was trying to bring together the smaller Republican parties on to a common platform. With the political wind so strongly behind him, Azaña, in November, then proposed that the now newly enlarged Liberal grouping should form an electoral alliance with the PSOE. Largo Caballero, swayed by the clear evidence of popular enthusiasm for such a pact, agreed finally after a special representative of the Comintern, the French Communist Jacques Duclos, helped to persuade him of its political necessity.

The Republican-Socialist agreement (expanded to include POUM, Syndicalists and the PCE) which emerged from these negotiations was limited to an electoral pact. Beyond this, all that Largo Caballero would agree to was to give parliamentary support to a Popular Front government; he wanted no repetition of the 'mistakes' of 1931–33 and he would not agree to Socialists participating in government. This refusal to give full co-operation was to undermine the authority of the Popular Front government and to exacerbate conservative fears that the Socialists were really aiming at revolution. The Popular Front electoral programme was liberal, not socialist. Its main call was for an amnesty for political prisoners and a return to the Republic of 14 April 1931, an implicit promise to revive the social legislation which Centre-Right governments had allowed to lapse during the previous two years.

The electoral agreement did nothing to heal the bitter divisions within the Socialist Party. Throughout Spain, the local strength of individual party leaders decided the selection of candidates. In the North, Prieto's hold remained firm, whereas the *caballeristas** dominated the South. With Prieto theoretically still in exile, Largo Caballero made the running in the election campaign, developing in his speeches two main themes: the need for proletarian unity (not the Republican unity of the Popular Front) and for a transformation of capitalist society, although carefully making clear that the revolution lay in the future. Socialism, he argued, could not be achieved within the framework of capitalist society and Prieto's confidence in reformism was totally misplaced.

Drawn by the election promise of amnesty, the anarchists wavered in their traditional allegiance to abstentionism. 'If we reaffirm abstentionism,' wrote Diego Abad de Santillán, 'we are giving victory to the dictatorship which wants to bring in Gil Robles and we will enter a fascist period with a legal look. If we declare ourselves in favour of voting, in order to consolidate the triumph of the left, we will be accused (even by the people on the left) of turning up our noses at our principles' [97 *p. 64*]. In the event the anarchists compromised by leaving out of their manifestos the traditional appeal 'Don't vote', and the election results, compared to

1933, were to show the effect of their new, albeit hesitant, attitude to political participation.

The Second Republic's electoral system differed profoundly from the English practice of single-member constituencies. Spain was divided into large electoral districts, with one deputy for each 50,000 voters. To get the best result, what was essential was to create unified lists of candidates, as the party alliance with a clear majority in each constituency received a built-in bonus. For example, in an electoral district entitled to return twenty deputies, a more than 50 per cent majority would secure the return of sixteen deputies from the winning list [36; 45]. The electoral advantage given to the Left by the Popular Front was not matched on the Right. As the head of the constitutionalist conservative party, Gil Robles was unwilling to ally himself on a national basis with the conspiratorial Right. However, he created local alliances where it was politically advantageous. He even offered a deal to José Antonio, the Falangist leader, who refused. A further complicating factor in the elections was the role of the caretaker Prime Minister, Portela Valladares, who was hoping to build up a Centre-Right faction in the Cortes which could hold the balance between Right and Left.

Electoral management was traditional in Spain, and the 1936 election was not markedly different from others. Portela Valladares, through the control of municipal councils, exercised a good deal of political patronage and was well placed to falsify electoral returns. In Lugo, Paul Preston writes, Portela was unassailable [36]. Time-honoured techniques of electoral control were used, ranging from the arrest of known Republicans (in Chite) to closing the polling stations an hour and a half before time. Such tactics may help to explain the strange case of twenty villages where no left-wing votes were recorded at all. Seventy-two per cent of the electorate voted, and the result was a narrow victory for the Popular Front. Anarchist abstentions were most marked in rural Spain, particularly in the Cádiz-Seville-Málaga triangle, where the turn-out fell to around 55 per cent. The Popular Front gained 34.3 per cent of the recorded votes; the Right, 33.2 per cent and the Basque Nationalists 5.4 per cent. The Socialists had 88 seats, the Republican parties (Republican Left and Republican Union) gained 113 seats. Of the smaller parties, the PCE had 16, and POUM and the Syndicalists had each returned a member. On the Right, CEDA had 101, the monarchists (including Calvo Sotelo), with 13 seats, had fewer than the Carlists' 15. The Falange had failed even to secure the election of its leader. The Radical Party, with only nine deputies, had virtually disappeared. To have a majority, the Popular Front needed 237 deputies. The workings of the electoral law gave them 263, with 133 to the Right and 77 to the Centre. What was abundantly clear was that no electoral mandate had been given for revolutionary change, either to Right or Left. All that could be said was that a Cortes had been elected with permission to govern, something no longer easy to achieve in the Spring of 1936.

THE REPUBLIC IN DANGER

The election results brought no balm to the right-wing parties. Gil Robles and CEDA had hoped to repeat the electoral success of 1933, and then, with a clear majority, to remodel the Republic's constitution. For the conservative leader the electoral defeat was a further political setback. In the December (1935) political crisis, his hopes of political power had been frustrated when the President had not invited him to form a government but instead had called for a general election. Gil Robles had then approached the Army for support, but General Fanjul, a fanatical member of the *Unión Militar Española* (UME),* had judged the time unsuitable for military intervention. When the results of the election were declared, Gil Robles proposed to the caretaker Prime Minister that he should allow him to head a new government as a means of winning over the Right. All that Portela wanted, however, was to get out as quickly as he could, and hand over to Azaña. In the months that followed, therefore, both the 'legal' Right and the extreme Right were seeking ways of saving Spain from what they saw as 'bolshevisation'.

Nothing in Azaña's reform policies justified so catastrophist an interpretation of the dangers threatening Spain. The Azaña government, which came to power in February 1936, comprised liberal middle-class Republicans, with a policy in line with the Popular Front manifesto: broadly a return to the programme of 1931–33. No Marxist was in the government. The Republicans' Socialist allies were unwilling (or like Prieto unable) to share power, split as they were between *prietistas*, moderate and reformist, and *caballeristas*, committed to a Marxist belief in a proletarian revolution at some ill-defined point in the future. The difference in the rank-and-file approach mirrored the attitude of the leaders: Prieto, militant revolutionary in 1934, was now committed to constitutionalism; while Largo Caballero was trying to build himself up as the 'Spanish Lenin'. The UGT leader's obstructive tactics in blocking Prieto's membership of the Azaña government contributed to the fatal weakening of that government's authority in the months before the Rising of 18 July.

Although dependent in the Cortes on the Socialist vote, the Republican government at least had Azaña's political authority to maintain it. But the Socialists decided to remove the President, thereby paving the way for the elevation of Azaña to the Presidency. Alcalá Zamora, the ousted President, had, after all, helped usher in the Republic. As a conservative and Catholic Republican he could be seen as a counterbalance to anti-clerical liberals or reforming socialists. However, he had bitterly offended the conservatives in December 1935 by his refusal to ask Gil Robles to form a government. He had maintained the integrity of the constitution against what he saw as an authoritarian threat and might reasonably, therefore, look to liberals for support. By his decision to call a general election he had given the Republicans and the Left an opportunity to take office. Yet in the move to force him out of office, he had no allies to whom he could look. The constitution permitted the Cortes to challenge the use of the Presidential prerogative after he had dissolved it twice. This prerogative the Left chose to exercise. 'Largo Caballero', writes Hugh Thomas 'hoped to remove Alcalá Zamora from office and then Azaña...by promoting his presidential candidature.' 'Prieto', he adds, 'was persuaded to take the lead' [85 *p. 171*]. Paul Preston on the other hand, writes of Prieto's 'campaign to depose Alcalá Zamora' [36 *p. 184*]. If Prieto's campaign had as its aim a new government with himself as its head, his drive to remove the President was extremely dangerous. On any political calculation, the removal of the President might be read as the preliminary to other major changes in a socialist direction. Yet Prieto clearly did not intend this, as is shown by his Cuenca speech on 1 May, when he warned of the danger of a military take-over if there was continued talk of revolution. In short, the motives of Prieto, in this key episode, remain extremely obscure.

On 7 April the Cortes voted by 238 votes to five to remove the President. The small vote against reflects right-wing abstention. On 8 May Azaña took over the Presidency and Casares Quiroga, who was certainly no strong man, became Prime Minister.

In the spring of 1936 the replacement of an experienced and respected Catholic President with a liberal politician responsible for the reduction of the Army and for the legislation touching the Church which so bitterly offended Catholic Spain might seem to be political lunacy. However, the main criticism made by the Right was not of the new Prime Minister as such, but of the lack of authority of his government, which was shown by the extent of public disorder. One obvious example of what right-wingers regarded as a collapse of authority was a wave of strikes. Madrid suffered not only from strikes in the building industry, but also from deadly rivalry between the UGT and CNT. In a free market economy strikes are an extreme form of collective bargaining, and the Spanish government, by using arbitration machinery, eventually arrived at a compromise with the UGT, though not the CNT. Far more difficult to deal with was the violence in the streets. Young militants clashed in demonstrations or at political meetings. The Falange was particularly active in street warfare, thereby justifying the claim made by the Right that Spain had no effective government.

In the countryside, there was another form of disorder. In some provinces such as impoverished Extremadura, the rural poor had occupied landlords' estates without any government action being taken to stop them. Such movements by land-hungry peasants seemed to require long-term solutions rather than a strengthening of the Civil Guard. Yet Spain, within living memory, only a decade earlier, had had a 'golden age' of civil peace under the rule of the 'iron surgeon', Primo de Rivera. Perhaps another Primo could bring peace and justice to Spain, end strikes, lawlessness and violence?

To Gil Robles a return to a military regime looked to be the only real alternative, since his own political ambitions to create a corporativist Spain by parliamentary means had been frustrated by his failure to achieve power. Within the Army itself, the Popular Front victory stimulated conspiracy and Gil Robles began to prepare his provincial supporters to co-operate with the Army when the military rising began. This co-operation, as Gil Robles later declared, was based on 'secret orders for collaboration' and on 'economic assistance, taken in appreciable quantities from the party's electoral funds' – a reference to the 500,000 pesetas which Gil Robles handed over to General Mola from CEDA funds [36 *p. 193*].

'The impetus of the conspiracy', writes Raymond Carr, 'came from a minority of junior officers, the only group in the Army with any sympathy with the Falangists' [54 *p. 67*]. This nuclear group was the *Unión Militar Española*,* a junta or committee, founded in 1933, comprising middle-rank officers, passionately anti-Left and linked with *africanistas* like Goded, Mola, and Franco. On 17 February, immediately after the Popular Front election victory, the UME in Madrid had answered General Fanjul's call to be ready to act, a call which the cautious Franco, however, rejected. With a Popular Front government actually in office, the UME rapidly expanded. Stanley Payne estimates that 'nearly half the officers on active duty' were members [15 *p. 317*]. The danger of a military rebellion was not ignored by the Republican government, but Azaña saw the real threat as coming from high-ranking career officers, particularly those well known for their strong nationalist anti-Republican or anti-Left views. To meet this danger from the Army, Azaña moved Franco to Tenerife, Goded to the Balearics, and Mola from Morocco to Pamplona. General Fanjul was retired. Before the dispersal began, however, these senior officers met together in Madrid and made a vague commitment to support a rebellion.

In General Mola the young officers found an organiser, while their figurehead was General Sanjurjo, now in exile in Portugal. From his base in Pamplona, Mola made soundings throughout the Spanish garrisons in the peninsula and in North Africa. His plan turned upon the immediate support of the mainland garrison forces which would mount an attack upon Madrid, the heartland of Spanish liberalism and socialism, and therefore the key to ultimate success. With Madrid under control, Mola assumed that organised resistance would quickly collapse. A new military government would then set about dealing with the problems left by the defeated parliamentary regime.

In essence, Mola's plan had much in common with the traditional *pronunciamiento*. Where it differed was in the contacts made with political groups, for Mola realised that a simple *pronunciamiento* was now an anachronism. His contacts ran from Gil Robles to Serrano Súñer, Franco's brother-in-law and a CEDA deputy, who in turn made contact with José Antonio. In the past the Falange had been contemptuous of the Army as a force for change but José Antonio began now to instruct local Falangist units to support the Rising. The most difficult political group to woo were the Carlists, with their commitment to a Carlist Pretender, but by 12 July they too had fallen in behind Mola, with a promise of a Carlist militia of 7,000 *requetés*. All that Mola now needed was an event which would give clear justification for rebellion. Twin assassinations in Madrid provided this opportunity.

On the evening of 12 July the first assassination took place. Lieutenant José Castillo, a socialist member of the Assault Guards, was shot down as he left his home. In the early hours of the 13th, Captain Condés of the Civil Guard, a close friend, set out to take revenge. He went first to the home of Gil Robles (who had withdrawn across the frontier with his family) and then to that of Calvo Sotelo, where he invited the monarchist leader to come to headquarters. On the way Calvo Sotelo was shot in the back of the head and his body delivered to the East Cemetery in Madrid. The murder of the monarchist leader while in the custody of the state's security forces could well be interpreted as evidence of the breakdown of public order, and Calvo Sotelo's murder triggered off the rebellion. From Pamplona, Mola dispatched telegrams fixing 18 July as the day.

PART TWO: THE CIVIL WAR 1936–39

3 THE MILITARY RISING

Although the Military Rising had the great advantage of surprise and the backing of the majority of younger officers throughout mainland Spain, it fell far short of its immediate objective: to take all Spain's major cities prior to an attack on the capital itself. Up to the beginning of July, General Franco, exiled in the Canaries, had vacillated before finally deciding that a rebellion could be justified. With his decision made, he insisted that the Rising should be for 'Spain without a label' – that is, that no commitment should be made to the political form that the new post-Rising regime would take. The method of making a revolution had a peculiarly Spanish look, sanctified by a long nineteenth-century Army tradition: a *pronunciamiento*, then a rising of the Army in provincial Spain, followed by the fall of the capital. This pattern was followed in 1936, but the timetable, scheduled to start on 18 July, had to be put forward because the plot had been discovered.

The Rising began, prematurely, at Melilla (in Spanish Morocco), when the conspiracy was betrayed to the authorities. The conspirators acted ruthlessly in removing actual and potential opponents in both the Army and the civilian population – a technique which, so often in the early days of the Rising, was to bring instant success – and first Melilla, and then Tetuán, the capital of Spanish Morocco, fell. General Franco was already on his way from Tenerife, airlifted in a plane chartered by Luis Bolín, a right-wing Spanish journalist living in London. As a cover, Hugh Pollard, the pilot, took his daughter and her friend as passengers, ostensibly going on holiday together. Franco arrived at Tetuán on 19 July to take command of the Army of Africa, which was Spain's élite military force.

On the mainland, the Rising first began in the South [*Doc. 2*]. In Seville, General Queipo de Llano, with great panache and daring, and almost single-handed, established military control of the centre of the city. Other towns in western Andalusia – Cádiz, Jérez and

Córdoba – also fell to the insurgents, often after protracted fighting. The commitment of the local Army garrisons to the rebellion, and also the willingness of the security forces, the Civil Guards and the Assault Guards, to abandon their allegiance to the Republic, were often the deciding factors. Where Army and police worked together, the military and civil arms of the Republican state collapsed, and the Madrid government was left with no means by which to restore control. In northern Spain, Saragossa, a major anarchist stronghold, fell almost without bloodshed, and in Oviedo the military governor, after reducing expected opposition by sending on a contingent of armed miners to defend Madrid, declared for the Rising, thus extinguishing the possibility of a repetition of 1934.

The 1923 military take-over which had placed Primo de Rivera in power began in Barcelona, with the backing of Catalan industrialists. Catalonia, with its diversified, productive industry was essential for the immediate success of the rebellion. From the Balearics – which, with the exception of Ibiza, had been secured for the Nationalists – General Goded flew into Barcelona to take charge of the Army contingents there. Troops moved into the centre of the city, where they came up against resistance from loyal Republican Assault Guards and the *Generalitat*'s own security forces, backed by the CNT militia [126]. As Raymond Carr argues, here the decisive factor was the intervention of the Civil Guard, who, late on the 19 July, came out for the Republic [54]. Further south, in left-wing Valencia, the local commander, General Martínez Monje, was a practised fence-sitter in a city where the rebellion was led by Major Barba, national organiser for the UME. However, taking his cue from events in Barcelona, the Valencian commander came out on 20 July for the Republic.

In Madrid there was some confusion amongst the Army plotters as to who was to lead the rebellion. Finally, the initiative was seized by General Fanjul, who locked himself, together with 2,500 supporters, in the Montana barracks, which on the afternoon of 19 July came under siege from workers' militias. Officers with left-wing connections – some of them members of the *Unión Militar Republicana Antifascista*,* a group set up in 1934 to counter the activities of UME – had already tried to issue arms to worker militants. On the 19th the government gave its approval to this action, and the militias who stormed the barracks on the 20th were armed with a variety of weapons, including artillery. When the barracks finally fell, many of the defenders were massacred although Fanjul himself was saved for later court-martial and execution.

By 20 July that partition of Spain which was to determine much of the early course of the war had already been established. The rebels controlled western Andalusia, Galicia, western Aragon, the towns of northern Castile, Extremadura and Navarre. Already major centres of working-class resistance such as Seville, Corunna and Granada, had fallen, and once this had happened normal working-class tactics were useless against an enemy which simply shot strikers, or, like Queipo de Llano, used the Moors to winkle out resisters in working-class districts of Seville. These towns could only be regained by prompt and intelligent military action, not readily forthcoming from a Republic divided by political conflicts.

Nevertheless only one major city, Seville, had fallen to the rebels; all the other great towns, centres of industry like Bilbao or ports like Santander, Málaga and Valencia, were still under the control of the government. Time, it might be argued, was on the side of the Republic, for the Nationalists, who were already short of arms, had no industries under their control. Furthermore, the majority of senior officers in the Army had remained loyal – only four of the twenty-four major-generals had gone over to the rebels. Where the Republic had failed was in retaining the loyalty of the junior officers, of whom more than two-thirds had joined the conspirators.

The military balance, if the security forces are included, was fairly equal, with the Army of Africa, consisting of 24,000 élite troops, representing in numbers and in equipment and skill the key to the situation. But that Army was still in North Africa, and the Spanish Navy, after a series of mutinies, was in the hands of the government, together with the Air Force. For the Republic, the clear need was to blockade the Straits, in order to prevent the Army of Africa from crossing, and to take the initiative by launching attacks upon the lightly held areas of the rebel command.

Within Republican Spain clear concerted action was even less easy now than in the recent past when the only difficulties had been regional obduracy, slowness of communications, and entrenched economic and social interests. Regionalism in Catalonia was now reinforced by the proliferation of anti-fascist committees and workers' militias, and in other provinces the controlling power was usually a Junta of the different political parties in that area, represented according to their varying strengths. In the capital, the government presided over a city where the UGT, the CNT and the PCE not only had their own policies and committees, but also their own drumhead court-martials. The central government's power of swift decision was dependent upon its capacity to deal tactfully with the different political factions. Furthermore, the sense that what was fundamental was the social and political revolution – a sense which differed in intensity from the Basque Provinces (where it hardly existed at all), to Catalonia (where, at first, most anarchists were certain that the revolution should take precedence over victory in war) – made the government's task a doubly delicate one. To this must be added the conviction, widespread except amongst the communists, that the military discipline necessary to fight a war was anathema to committed revolutionaries, and that such discipline had brought working-class brothers into the rebellion on the Nationalist side who would otherwise have been friends of the Republic.

Faced by the division of Spain and by the call to arms for the people from trade unions and left-wing political parties, Prime Minister Casares Quiroga panicked and resigned, to be replaced by a Left Republican, Martínez Barrio. He in turn was challenged by Largo Caballero, who refused to support a government with Martínez Barrio at its head. On the night of 18 July the new Prime Minister telephoned Mola in Pamplona, inviting him to take the Ministry of War in a new government as the first step towards a compromise settlement. Mola, however, refused. Why did he do so, when by accepting he might have averted civil war?

In Navarre, with the Carlist *requetés* ready to 'liberate' Madrid, with enthusiasts ready for a new crusade, arguably Mola might have found it impossible to hold back the forces he had unleashed, as indeed Martínez Barrio might have had profound difficulty in persuading the CNT in Catalonia to turn back the revolution and submit to a new coalition government, dominated by class enemies and erstwhile rebels. Perhaps Mola's comment to Martínez Barrio that 'neither of us can control the masses' was fair. He went on to repeat the new rightist doctrine that 'the Popular Front cannot keep order', which was now tragically true of the Spain that Mola and his fellow conspirators had helped to create. On Mola, however, must rest the responsibility for refusing to seek a way out of what was clearly a stalemate. Following the failure of his attempt at compromise, Martínez Barrio resigned, since he was unwilling to agree to the distribution of arms to workers' militias – a policy which, by encouraging the formation of armed forces outside the control of the constituted authorities, would have alarmed the middle classes. Martínez Barrio was replaced by José Giral, an Azañista, formerly a professor of chemistry in Madrid University, who promptly ordered the distribution of arms so as to help establish a volunteer militia, which, together with loyalist military and para-military forces, could defend the capital against the expected attack.

That first attack was launched from Pamplona on 19 July, and got as far as the Somosierra Pass, in the Guadarrama mountains to the north of Madrid. In the original plan, two other forces were to converge on Madrid, one from Valladolid and the other from Saragossa, but Goded's failure to capture Barcelona prevented the forces from Saragossa taking part, as they stayed to defend their town against possible attack from Catalonia. The Valladolid column reached the Alto de León Pass on 22 July, but there it was halted by a militia force brought hurriedly up from Madrid. Both Passes were the scene of bitter and costly fighting, as a consequence of which the Republican line was finally held on the Madrid side of these entries to the capital. Mola's forces were now desperately short of ammunition. The grand plan to take Madrid from the north had failed, and as a consequence the front was stabilised for the remainder of the war [68].

With Mola's forces held in the mountains north of Madrid, the second attack came from General Franco's forces, mainly airlifted from North Africa in the newly acquired Junkers transport planes (see page 48). As the Army of Africa moved towards the capital, Franco ordered three columns to be diverted to relieve the rebel forces at Toledo, where Colonel José Moscardó, together with officers, Civil Guards, Falangists, dependants, and around 100 hostages, had withdrawn into the Alcázar, the old fortress which dominates the city. The Alcázar had been sniped at in a desultory fashion, and occasionally bombarded by the besieging Republicans. On 27 September, the Nationalist forces entered the city, ending the siege and relieving Moscardó and his men. The Republican militia were slaughtered; even the wounded in hospital were disposed of by grenades thrown amongst them [60]. This symbolic victory, in Spain's most Christian city, could be taken as an implicit promise that those who risked all for Franco (or Spain) would not be forgotten or overlooked. Toledo was a great propaganda victory for Franco, propelling him on to the world stage through press and cinema coverage. He was already identified internationally as the leader of the rebellion, after his election as Supreme Commander, Generalissimo, on 21 September. On the day that the Nationalists entered the Alcázar, the 28th, the Army leaders made Franco 'Head of the Government of the Spanish State' – a title that he immediately shortened to the more potent 'Head of the Spanish State'. Franco's political career had begun.

Later, Franco was to admit that he had committed a military error in relieving Toledo, but that it had been politically necessary. General Kindelán had warned Franco that the relief of Toledo might lose him Madrid, and in the event the delay gave the Republic time to bring in Russian advisers and Russian equipment before the attack on the capital was launched.

The 'liberation' of Madrid began in November with an assault on the north-west of the city through the University suburb, where resistance from the Madrid middle class might be expected to be fairly light. When the assault began on 8 November, the defenders included not only the Communist Fifth Regiment, a crack fighting force, but the Durruti column from Aragon and the first contingents of the International Brigade. Morale was not helped by the exodus of Largo Caballero's government to Valencia, but the organisation of defence was made easier by the consequent removal of the Spanish bureaucracy and the concentration of military authority in the hands of General Miaja. The Nationalist attack was accompanied by massive air raids upon Madrid, the first use in Europe of terror bombing, and an ominous predictor for the future. The early days of the siege were also marred by the murder of more than a thousand Nationalist political prisoners who, ostensibly, were being transferred from the Model prison to a prison near the Barajas airport. This massacre was 'justified' by General Mola's famous remark to visiting journalists that Madrid's capture would be helped by a 'Fifth Column' of secret Nationalist supporters in the capital.

One tactic which would have relieved the pressure on the town would have been the deployment of the 10,000 Asturian miners concentrated around Oviedo to attack Mola's forces from the rear. Nothing perhaps more dramatically illustrates the strength of localism – or even the influence of history – than the record of the use of militia forces in the Asturias. At the beginning of the Military Rising, Colonel Aranda, the officer in charge, had taken Oviedo by a ruse. Pretending at first to support the Republic, he had then declared for the Nationalists and made ready to defend Oviedo against the miners from the surrounding districts. Almost to a day, on the anniversary of the October 1934 Revolt, the Asturian militias attacked the town and battled their way to the centre, suffering heavy losses as they did so. When relief columns from Galicia arrived, the Asturian militia were forced to retreat, but they kept up a stubborn siege of the town until the final collapse of the Northern front in 1937 [126]. Yet Oviedo was not of major military significance, and the effort expended in besieging it was largely wasted. The whole episode displayed the strength of localism, the close loyalties of the Asturian miners, and most vividly the fundamental weakness of the Republic – namely the absence of an overriding command and the lack of commitment to the overall military requirements of the Republic. In fact, during these early years, the Republic's supporters were engaged not in one war but in a series of local wars, each organised and run by differing – and sometimes hostile – groups.

The defence of Madrid was a heavy charge on the Republic and George Hills has argued that it might have made more military sense to abandon the capital, thereby forcing the Nationalists to control a mainly hostile city [68]. All supplies for Madrid had to come overland from Valencia, with the major routes from Barcelona and Bilbao, which were both ports and industrial centres, held by the enemy. The argument for abandonment, however, overlooks the ruthlessness of Nationalist repression, displayed most ferociously when Madrid finally fell, and the great psychological value of possessing the capital city of Spain. To the foreign journalist, to liberal opinion outside Spain, Madrid could be seen as the front line in the battle against international fascism, and its defence a charge, if only psychological, upon the whole of the democratic world.

How, then, was Madrid saved in the first onslaught on the city? Of the confusion and disorder in the capital, there is ample evidence. H. E. Knoblaugh, the American journalist, paints a picture of 'a continuous thinning of the Loyalist volunteer ranks' and of militia men deserting their posts and returning without authority to their homes [131]. The initial defence of Madrid was clearly a haphazard affair, with the Junta responsible for Madrid's defence able to exercise little overall control of militia units. Yet Madrid held out. Was it due, as General Franco contended, to 'the shock troops of international communism', the International Brigades, and to the volume of Soviet material arriving in Spain in October? Russian support is obviously of prime importance, yet two other factors were also on the side of the defenders. Henry Buckley, the English journalist, argues strongly that 'it was the courage and sacrifice of the Madrid people which alone held the feeble lines which separated Franco from the city' [122 *p. 263*] [*Doc. 10*]. On the other hand, George Hills and Raymond Carr rest their case on the number of volunteers available for the city's defence. Hills gives a figure of 8,000 as the maximum for the attackers, against 'at least 40,000 men-at-arms within Madrid' and 'possibly as many as 100,000' [68 *p. 86*]. 'Men-at-arms' may be an exaggerated description of some of the sections, given the inadequacy of their equipment. Raymond Carr gives the more modest estimate of 23,000. He argues, however, that Madrid's successful defence rested on the fact that 'throughout the battles of Madrid, the government had more men and materials than the Nationalists' [*54 p. 158*].

If the attackers were relatively few, Franco behaved with his well-known 'prudence' in not sending in any reserves he may have had. Had his 'prudence' deserted him in attacking so strongly held a city with an inadequate force? Had he, perhaps, been misinformed about the mood inside Madrid? Was he over-committed to the political value of capturing the capital? Whatever judgement is made upon the battle of Madrid, all the contemporary evidence points to the willingness of its citizens to sacrifice their lives in defending it. Without popular support, the International Brigades would have been too small to hold the city; without civilian stubbornness in the face of air raids and military bombardment, resistance in Madrid would have collapsed.

The reinforcement of both sides from external sources was a significant development: Spain's Civil War now had an international dimension. The arrival of Russian supplies was of great importance to the Republican militia in Madrid. Soviet tanks were now readily available, although effective personnel to deploy them were in desperately short supply [155]. Again, Soviet fighter aircraft gave the Republic air superiority for the first time.

In November, the German Condor Legion disembarked at Cadiz, an élite force with the latest military equipment that Germany could assemble: fighter and bomber aircraft, together with tanks and other motorised units. The Spanish Civil War was beginning to have an importance beyond the peninsula as a testing ground for the latest weapons and tactics.

In all, 12,000 Germans came, a military presence that Franco continued to deny existed at all. The Germans had complained of the 'hesitant and routine procedures' which had prevented the capture of Madrid, and Franco had had to accept the terms on which this further assistance was provided: that it would be controlled by a German officer (Colonel Wolfram von Richthofen) and that there would be a more active conduct of the war. The Condor Legion was responsible for the terror bombing of the capital which was a new and terrible extension of the fighting.

The fall of Málaga in February 1937 illustrated all the problems which harassed the Republic in the early days of the war-inept military and civil leadership – warring political factions and the unwillingness of another region (Valencia) to send assistance. Málaga was linked to Republican Spain by a narrow coastal road to Almería, and the surrounding countryside was dominated by the CNT. Since the Rising, Málaga had suffered from the savage settlement of personal scores, and an outbreak of church burning. The attack on Málaga was essentially an Italian affair. Mussolini, through his local commander, General Roatta, had pushed Franco into accepting his concept of a lightning campaign against this important Andalusian city. Franco preferred (in keeping with his doctrine of *limpieza**) a slow advance which would enable the Nationalists to 'cleanse', that is kill, all Republican sympathisers as his army moved forward. When Málaga was captured, Franco displayed little enthusiasm. To Mussolini's proposal that, from Málaga, the CTV* would sweep up the coast to capture Valencia, the seat of the Republican government, Franco was markedly cool.

Even the suggestion from his own general in Seville, Queipo de Llano, that his forces should attack the coastal town of Almería to the north of Málaga, was vetoed. Franco's thinking here was political rather than military. He had no wish to boost the stock of de Llano – the Generalissimo had an almost paranoiac conviction that he was surrounded by political rivals – nor did he want the capital to be delivered into his hands by a foreign army. As Paul Preston points out [155], for the Republicans one windfall of the Italian victory was a highly optimistic assessment of the effectiveness of the Italian forces made by both Franco and Mussolini, but not shared by their commanding officer, General Roatta.

With Nationalist victory came bloody repression. Republican sympathisers were murdered, some summarily, others after a rapid trial and an equally rapid execution. Nearly 4,000 Republicans were killed in the first week alone. The loss of this major Andalusian town produced much bitter recrimination in the Republican ranks. The communists searched for a scapegoat and pointed the finger at General Asensio, Largo Caballero's closest military adviser.

Málaga's fall coincided with a fresh Nationalist offensive on the Madrid front. Franco's strategy was simple and potentially extremely dangerous: to cut the Madrid–Valencia highway by an attack up the valley of the Jarama. The attack was mounted by the Moors and the Foreign Legion. The capital's defence against such an experienced and skilful force was marred by incompetence and by in-fighting between the commanding Republican generals, Miaja and Pozas. It was distinguished, on the other hand, by the extraordinary tenacity and courage of the Internationals and by their very heavy casualties. The British Battalion lost one-third of its members in the battle, including the young writer Christopher Caudwell.

The Americans in the Abraham Lincoln Battalion had their first major experience of the disasters of war, celebrated in the Brigade song [59]. Russian aircraft, Chatos, proved their superiority to the Junkers of the Condor Legion, and Russian tanks held up the Moors' advance on the ground. In the end, the battle was inconclusive and both sides dug in for a long war of attrition.

The next month saw the opening of another attempt to take the capital and to complete the encirclement begun at Jarama. The attack came from the north-east of the city, and was aimed at Guadalajara. It became famous as the first major battle in which Italian 'volunteers', 30,000 in all, took part, superbly equipped with new mechanised units, mobile artillery, armoured cars, lorries, fighter and reconnaissance aeroplanes. The engagement was intended to be a splendid showpiece for Fascist Italy's new army, and to give to all potential foes a demonstration of its high standards. In support of the Italians were 15,000 Nationalists. The Italians, however, came up against determined resistance, strengthened by the heavy Russian tanks, which were superior to the light tanks of the CTV [58]. They also had to contend with freezing cold and roads turned to slush. The battle was not without its tragic irony, for the Fascist volunteers found themselves fighting their fellow countrymen in the Garibaldi Battalion of the International Brigades. For the Italians, Guadalajara was a disaster, politically and militarily. They were later to claim that their Spanish allies on the Nationalist side had given them no support.

The overall battle plan, understood by Roatta to be with the agreement of General Franco, was based upon a combined offensive. The Nationalists would attack in the Jarama valley, coinciding with the Italian offensive against Guadalajara on 8 March. No Nationalist movement took place at all. To Mussolini, Franco offered a variety of lame explanations, of which the simplest was that there had been a muddle over dates. The Italians were left to bear the brunt of the fighting and the consequent humiliation. Certainly there was some wry amusement amongst the 'backward' Spaniards at the defeat inflicted upon the Italian army. For the first time the world saw the extent of Italian involvement in Spain and the charade of non-intervention when Soviet equipment was pitted against Italian or German. Guadalajara, like Jarama, ended in stalemate, with heavy losses to both sides.

The Nationalists had assumed the almost immediate fall of

Madrid, and with the failure of their efforts to secure overall control of Spain, the capture of the capital became their major strategical objective. The heavy fighting in the capital's suburbs and on the perimeter of the city had underlined how difficult such a strategy would be to maintain. After Guadalajara, Franco abandoned this objective and settled down to whittling away the Republican zone area by area, returning to attack Madrid only in the last days of the war.

One major consequence of the failure to take Madrid was Franco's decision to build a new army, based upon conscription, ready for the long, humanly costly war which he saw ahead.

4 THE INTERNATIONALISATION OF THE WAR

The Rising had clearly not been a total success, and the despairing Mola was contemplating suicide. Without assistance from foreign sources, the Rising might have petered out into a negotiated settlement. The military balance rested with the Army of Africa, Spain's élite force, but this was stranded in North Africa. Hitler's intervention, taken on his own initiative, was to save the day for the Nationalists and make possible not only the ultimate defeat of the Republic but also Franco's emergence as the new leader of the rebels.

Franco, still in North Africa, sent two emissaries – the German Nazis, Adolf Langenheim and Johannes Bernhardt – to Berlin to seek help from their fellow countrymen. The two envoys had for many years been in contact with the *Ausland-Organisation* (AO) in Berlin, the agency responsible for Germans living abroad. Bernhardt himself was well known to many *africanistas* as a businessman involved with the Spanish Army in Morocco. Ángel Viñas has unravelled the chain which led these two men to Hitler [89]. In Berlin their first contact was with Bohle, head of the AO, who jumped at the opportunity to play a major role in events and rang Rudolf Hess who then sent his private plane to bring the two emissaries to him, and then rang Hitler. By 10 o'clock on the evening of 25 July the two AO men from North Africa were presenting Franco's letter to Hitler. In such a way was Franco's fortune made, by a chain of communication stretching from the AO in Morocco to the Führer in Bayreuth. A different fate befell Mola's plea for help, which got bogged down in the recesses of the German Foreign Office.

Hitler went far beyond the modest request Franco had made for fighters and anti-aircraft guns. Circumventing the German Foreign Office, he ordered 20 Junkers 52 transport planes to Morocco on the strict condition that they were to be sent direct to Franco and to be placed under his immediate control. On 29 July these transport planes arrived in Morocco and began that transport of the Army of

Africa to the mainland which gave the Nationalists a new and experienced striking force. Subsequently, Hitler gave different reasons for his prompt intervention, ranging from the danger of communism in Spain to the German need to see a friendly power in control of the straits. Occasionally he would refer to the strategic importance of Spain's minerals. Ángel Viñas [89] argues that there is sufficient evidence to show that Hitler's primary purpose in intervening was a matter of long-term diplomatic and strategic considerations – to ensure a pro-German government in Madrid which by its presence would limit France's political and military options – and that in his Spanish policy Hitler was following the political line begun by the occupation of the Rhineland in March 1936.

Unlike Hitler, Mussolini had already dabbled in Spanish politics. He had given financial assistance to a proposed monarchist rising in 1934 and he put José Antonio on his payroll. Franco's agent, Luis Bolín, first met the Italian Foreign Minister, Count Ciano, who was strongly in favour of sending help, but it needed the arrival of a well-known Spanish monarchist to back up Bolín to persuade Mussolini to take action, albeit reluctantly, for he had not yet worked out clearly what his foreign policy was to be. Later, he was to justify his intervention in various ways – as a means of preventing the establishment of a communist state in Spain, for instance; or as a way of sharpening the Italian fighting spirit now that the Ethiopian campaign was over. In the event, he committed himself to sending 12 Savoia bombers to Spain, a promise fulfilled when they left Sardinia for Morocco on 30 July.

For the Republic, immediate military supplies were far more difficult to come by. The Spanish Civil War divided opinion both in England and France. The British Left was committed to neutrality, yet strongly supported the sale of arms to Spain's legal government. Baldwin's National Government, on the other hand, came to see neutrality as requiring a ban on the sale of arms to both sides in the conflict. Information from Spain reaching English official sources talked of Soviet agents and built up a picture of a communist regime. As Jill Edwards observes, 'in the first weeks of the rebellion, it was the thread of anti-communism which formed the warp of British government attitudes' [61 *p. 3*]. To the British ruling class in the 1930s, Communism – and behind that the Soviet Union – seemed always to pose more of a threat than a resurgent Germany or an Italy vying with Britain for control of the Mediterranean. At least, in neither country had the established social order been overthrown, or property put at risk.

In France the situation was more complex. A new Centre-Left coalition, the Popular Front, had won the elections in April, and Leon Blum, a distinguished socialist, had formed France's first Popular Front government. This new coalition was intended to unite all those in France opposed to fascism. When the Madrid government turned to France for military aid, Blum immediately, on 22 July, promised to allow the sale of arms to Spain. The position in international law was clear: a constitutional government had an undisputed right to buy arms to suppress an internal revolt. On the French Left this legal argument was reinforced by a natural sympathy for a fellow Popular Front government, albeit still an entirely Liberal affair. There were sound strategic reasons as well. If the rebellion was successful, France would be caught in a vice between three fascist powers. A hostile Spain, furthermore, could threaten France's lifeline to her colonies in North and West Africa. Yet by 8 August Blum had reversed his position. No arms were to be sold to the Republican government. What had happened in that brief space of time to induce the Prime Minister and his government to change course?

Fernando de los Rios, the Republic's special envoy in Paris, reported as early as 25 July the almost universal hostility of the French press to the sale of armaments to the Republic. Furthermore, he referred to the French President's opinion that the arms for Spain might involve France in war or revolution. The French Right were vociferously supporting the Nationalists, and Blum came increasingly to share the President's expressed fear of civil war, which might leave France as another fascist state.

A further factor was the influence of the British. The Ambassador, Sir George Clerk, was pressing for a non-intervention agreement, and made no attempt to conceal his pro-Nationalist sympathies. The British view was that the rebels were the only force capable of defeating anarchy and Soviet influence.

That Blum was under very great pressure, within his Cabinet, from the President and from Britain during this time, is quite clear. A further weight in the balance was the influence of Sir Anthony Eden, the British Foreign Secretary. There was the hint that any wavering on the British policy on non-intervention might make future Anglo-French co-operation more difficult. The possibility that the slender life-line connecting the two countries might be even less able to bear the strain (and this not six months since Hitler's invasion of the Rhineland) helped push the French government towards this reversal of policy. On 8 August, as an alternative to supplying arms to the Madrid government, Blum proposed that the major powers should collectively agree to take no part in the Civil War and to ban the sale of armaments to either side. Britain, France, Germany, Italy and the Soviet Union were to enter into a non-intervention agreement as the basis for this joint policy. Non-intervention gave scope for fence-sitting of a unique kind. The Non-Intervention Committee was based in London, manned by the Foreign Office, chaired by an indecisive peer and continually circumvented by the Germans and Italians. One of the major paradoxes of the procedure was that only committee members could initiate discussions or submit evidence to the Committee. Since Spain was not a member, her government was debarred from bringing before the Committee evidence of continuing German and Italian intervention. Majorca, for instance, was almost an Italian colony during the war. At the battle of Guadalajara, the Spanish government had irrefutable evidence that some of the Italian 'volunteers' were in fact Italian regulars, but it had no effective means of submitting its proof to the Non-Intervention Committee. During the lifetime of the Committee, Britain and France countenanced the most blatant breach of the agreement by the other three powers: aircraft, tanks, artillery and personnel from the other three signatories flowed in during most of the war.

Why then did Blum change course? Why, if there was Anglo-French concern about possible Soviet influence in Spain, allow that influence to grow by giving a monopoly of the supply of arms to the Spanish Republic, thereby giving the Soviet Union a potential stranglehold on the Spanish government? No final answer can be given to the question why France took the course she did, albeit never with quite the same obvious preference for Franco that Britain displayed. One further argument is that in the summer of 1936, many observers thought that the Spanish Republic, with its improvised forces, could not hold out for very much longer against Franco's highly disciplined Army, that Madrid would soon fall and with the capital, the war would be lost. Would it be wise to assist what might soon be a defeated side? Again, there was the danger that the Spanish war might rapidly become a European war, in which any involvement by France would weaken her capacity to defend her southern frontier. Against this interpretation must be set the certainty that at no time during these crucial three weeks did the French government seek military advice on the strategic implications for France of the Civil War in Spain. Perhaps the most influential factor was that fear, voiced by the President, of a similar civil war breaking out in France, where the political balance was extremely delicate and political rivalries as intense as in Spain. The way would then be open to intervention from Germany, Italy and the Soviet Union – a danger Blum could in no circumstances risk. In this view, not only would the stability of the government be put in jeopardy by aid to Spain, but the future of France itself.

In consequence, the legitimate Spanish government could not officially buy arms at all – except from Mexico. This was an almost unprecedented situation for a lawful government to find itself in. Despite the vocal sympathy of Claud Bowers, the American Ambassador to Spain, Roosevelt's America also refused to sell arms to the Republic, President Roosevelt announcing 'a moral embargo' on arms sales to either side. However, the Texaco Oil Company gave long-term credits to the Nationalists [87]. That the Spanish government could only purchase its main supplies from the Soviet Union, and that by covert means, was a tragedy for Spain and eventually for Europe. This dependence was to bring her internal policy increasingly in line with Soviet wishes, which coincided initially with those of her government – a return to legalism and a halt to the revolution [93]. Before the eyes of the Non-Intervention Committee, the Italians and the Germans gave open assistance to the Nationalists. They tried out planes, tanks, motorised vehicles, tactics, all of which were – honed by use and improved by experience of battle – to be deployed against the Allies in the Second World War. On the other hand, the Soviet Union sent no regular troops, masquerading as volunteers, but built up an international network to supply arms. Krivitsky, the Russian defector, maintains that by the end of August 1936 Stalin had decided to send arms to Spain as part of a long-term Soviet policy to build a united front against Nazi Germany [70]. Within days, an apparatus based upon Arms Purchase Commissions in European capitals and supervised by the NKVD, the forerunner of the KGB, was set up to organise the purchase of arms – even from Germany itself. They were then despatched to Spain, often accompanied by invoices giving their source of origin as China or Latin America. The new Soviet initiative was symbolised in Spain by the appointment of the first Russian Ambassador, Marcel Rosenberg. Spain had recognised the Soviet regime as far back as 1933, but there had been no previous exchange of ambassadors, although the Popular Front government in February had agreed to this. Rosenberg was backed up by a Russian military mission, headed by General Jan Berzin, and by the arrival of groups of Russian experts. By the first weeks of

November there were around 500 experts, together with 100 tanks and 100 aircraft, both superior to Nationalist equipment, giving the Republic the technical equipment needed to defend the capital when Franco's assault began. The technical superiority of the Republic was only lost in 1937, when Germany began to supply new equipment, including the very fast fighter, the Messerschmidt 109.

Both Hitler and Stalin perceived the importance of Spain in any future international alignment and, more importantly, in any European war. Hitler was primarily concerned with the strategic implications of Nationalist victory, and in Britain this was an aspect of the Spanish conflict which the strategist Liddell Hart continually urged, in vain, on the British government. There were, he argued, clear dangers to Gibraltar and to North Africa in a Francoist Spain. Yet non-intervention remained Britain's answer. The significance of Britain's stance is best summed up by Jill Edwards in these words: 'By turning a blind eye both to the intervention of the dictators and to the need to protect British shipping to Spain, the British government aided Franco as decisively as if it had sent arms to him' [61 *p. 215*]. In 1936, however, British policy was more influenced by the possible threat of the expansion of Soviet power. It is, therefore, an additional paradox that, given Britain's underlying concerns, her policy of non-intervention produced in some degree the result which she most feared. It might be judged fortunate for her that Soviet involvement in the Spanish Civil War was not directed to creating a communist Spain – indeed almost the reverse – but to bolstering up its legitimate democratic government so that Spain could remain as a counter in international affairs and, with other Western democratic governments, become a possible ally in any future Nazi-Soviet conflict.

5 THE REPUBLIC – OR THE REVOLUTION?

After the Civil War, Franco claimed that the Rising had been a pre-emptive strike to prevent a left-wing take-over. Except within Nationalist propaganda, no such communist conspiracy had ever existed, yet one of the many ironies of Spain's Civil War was that the Army rebellion triggered off a Spanish revolution which was broadly anarchist rather than communist. Throughout Republican Spain, except in the Basque Provinces, the established authorities were swept aside and replaced by workers' committees. This revolutionary change affected both towns, where councils gave way to political parties and industry was run by collectives, and the countryside, where agrarian collectives were formed to organise farming and local services [*Doc. 3d*].

During the first year of the war, the Revolution became a key question in the political debates within the Republic. To liberals and many socialists the Revolution was divisive and could endanger success against the common enemy; it must therefore be halted, rolled back even, to permit a politically united people to concentrate on the prime objective of winning the war. To most anarchists, however, as to POUM in Catalonia, the Republic without the Revolution would be void of social content, a liberal political shell whose defence would not win hearts and minds. The problem of priorities was made more complex by the traditional anarchist attitude to all authority which did not spring from below. Anarchists were convinced that authority, by its very nature, impaired the dignity of the free man. Yet without it, how could an efficient military organisation be set up? [108; 113] [*Doc. 3*]

Prime Minister Giral's decision to dissolve the regular Army and to arm the working-class militias led to the formation of irregular armed groups, owing allegiance to their own local party branch and not to the distant, abstract Republic. Articulate, committed workers, faced with the need to defend their own lines, debated tactics and strategy. For the Republican government there were two related problems: how to secure recognition of the necessity of central government and how to weld the militias into an army with sufficient motivation (and equipment) to win the war.

In Catalonia the problem posed by 'dual power' was particularly acute, aggravated by a strongly entrenched regionalism which had shaded over into Catalan nationalism. Catalanism was largely a middle-class movement, bound up with language, culture and pride in Catalonia's great economic achievement, enriched by an awareness of her separate history. Working-class Catalans paid little heed to Catalanism. Their support was given to the most powerful workers' movement in Spain, mainly anarchist and CNT, but partly socialist and POUM. Within Catalonia there was a rapid burgeoning of village communes. In Barcelona itself, nearly all industry and services were run by workers' collectives. The civil authority, the *Generalitat*, was largely replaced by the Anti-Fascist Militia Committee, with its network of ministries. All major decisions affecting military policy, war industry, and the use of the militias, were made by the Anti-Fascist Militia Committee [50; 112].

The revolution in Catalonia created that euphoric sense of comradeship which George Orwell describes so vividly [135] [*Doc. 11*]. The revolution challenged, too, the male chauvinism so strongly entrenched in Spain. In some ways, the liberation of women took giant steps forward in Republican towns, although in the countryside attitudes changed hardly at all. In anarchist collectives in rural Aragon, for instance, little altered and 'the women's place was in the kitchen or working on the land' [126 *p. 288*]. The new freedom took the form of legalised abortion, birth-control information and sex-education classes. In the early days, women could also be found fighting in the militias, a form of equality abandoned after the battle of Guadalajara in March 1937, when women were then called on to help behind the lines in what were seen as traditional roles. In Spanish, and even in European terms, this openness about sex was revolutionary, and Spanish women have spoken to Ronald Fraser of the absence from male harassment on the streets, which was a consequence of the new relationship. A woman teacher in Madrid remembers that women were no longer 'objects but human beings'. Indeed, although there was no equality in terms of pay and no equality in the home, nevertheless this recognition of the fact that 'both sexes were humanly equal was one of the most remarkable social advances of the time' [126 *p. 286*] [*Doc. 13*].

The revolution's other face was less attractive. Working-class anti-clericalism was particularly fierce in Barcelona, as Rafael Shaw, an English journalist, had observed even in the early years of the twentieth century [21]. In the first weeks of the war, churches were closed, their treasures looted or destroyed, priests and monks arrested or shot. It was in Catalonia that the Republic's anti-religious face was most public and helped to give support to the widespread right-wing conviction that the Republic was godless. Again, traditional courts of law had been superseded by revolutionary justice, speedy and arbitrary, with political or class enemies permanently silenced. In the countryside, new village authorities took over the functions of the pre-Civil War councils.

To the moderate socialist leader, Prieto, the need to establish a Popular Front government which could command working-class loyalty was extremely urgent. Such a government would have to recommend itself to Britain and France as leading a democratic regime. The French communist newspaper *L'Humanité* (3 August 1936) summed up the dilemma facing Spain: 'the defence of Republican law and order through the respect for property' must be the new watchword. The only possible head of a Popular Front government, in Prieto's view, would be Largo Caballero, whose difficult task would be to turn back the revolution and re-establish a legal and bourgeois regime. Defeating the Franco threat must be shown to be more important than advancing the revolution. To the 'Spanish Lenin', then, would fall a truly Leninist task: uniting the country behind him to defeat the counter-revolutionaries. Everything would have to be sacrificed to winning the war; only after victory had been achieved could the revolution resume its advance. Marcel Rosenberg, the Russian Ambassador, continued to warn of the grave dangers of losing the façade of 'legality'. In Stalin's opinion, a 'Red' Spain would align Spain too obviously with the Soviet Union for the good of either country [50].

Largo Caballero came to power on 4 September, following the resignation of Giral, and he headed the first genuine Popular Front government. It was a broad coalition of Socialists and Communists and included five Liberals. The new government's political base was widened further when, on 4 November, four anarchists joined, including Garcia Oliver as Minister of Justice and as Minister of Health, Federica Montseny, the first woman to reach high office. This break with the anarchists' long-established refusal to participate in the normal constitutional arrangements greatly eased the working of the new policy of re-establishing republican legality (for anarchist-dominated committees now faced a government with anarchist members) and made continuing anarchist attachment to the revolution extremely difficult to sustain. As Abad de Santillán, an influential anarchist, later commented, 'We knew that it was not possible for the Revolution to triumph if we did not triumph in the war beforehand. We sacrificed the Revolution itself without understanding that this sacrifice also implied sacrificing the aims of the war' [113 *p. 43*].

The government's attack upon 'dual power' began immediately. In Catalonia the *Generalitat* began to resume control. The first step was to widen its membership by adding to it nine anarchists. This was followed by the dissolution of the Anti-Fascist Militia Committee. In October the Catalan government published a decree establishing its legal right to control the collectives. The first major test came in a confrontation with the Council of Aragon, an authority independent of the Catalan government, and dominated by Aragon anarchists. To secure its submission, the *Generalitat* appealed to Largo Caballero for his support, and by December he had forced the Council to come within the legal framework of the state system. The central government also defined the Council's membership in order to include liberals and communists, and laid down the extent of its powers. At village level anarchist committees were dissolved and replaced by councils sanctioned by the central government [101]. A similar process of returning Republican Spain to pre-war normality was adopted towards the farm collectives, a particular cause of irritation, as they were slow to carry out government orders and reluctant to pay taxes. The relationship of one collective with another and the structure of the collective itself depended entirely on local theory and practice [46; 109]. The work of disciplining these outcrops of revolutionary Spain was entrusted to Vicente Uribe, Communist Minister of Agriculture in the Popular Front government. By December 1936 he had created a Peasant Federation, committed to supporting peasant proprietorship, to lead the campaign against the rural collectives, particularly strong in Aragon [107]. In June 1937 a decree legalised collectives, and by implication gave the government the right to modify or destroy them. In some parts of Spain, trusted units of the Army were used to break up collectives. In eastern Aragon, where collectivisation was most widespread and where a higher percentage of land had been owned by grandees than elsewhere in Spain, it was reported by October 1937 that land was being returned to its original owners.

The Largo Caballero government, symbol of the victory of the popular forces in Spain, effectively carried through a policy of returning Spain to republican normality. In this policy the most

enthusiastic supporters were found in the PCE,* the Spanish
Communist Party, which had grown rapidly in size and influence
since the outbreak of the war. By the beginning of 1937, the party
had 250,000 members recruited across a wide social range.
Alongside 87,000 industrial workers and 62,000 rural workers,
there were 76,000 peasant landowners, 15,500 middle-class and
7,000 from the intellectual and professional classes. Its key policy
was defence of small property; its economic doctrine rested on the
market, on free enterprise for the peasantry. It campaigned to
transfer the expropriated estates of Nationalist supporters to the
peasantry – a policy which failed in the face of Socialist insistence
on nationalisation. It is ironic to contrast the PCE's defence of the
small peasantry, the rural petty bourgeoisie, with the deliberate
destruction of a similar class, the kulaks, by the Soviet Communist
Party [52 *p. 28*]. Communist policy during this period was also
directed to reducing the influence of elements which actually or
potentially diverged from the PCE line. The history of the
Communist Party in Catalonia illustrates this point. In July 1936,
four pro-Stalinist Catalan Marxist groups merged to form the PSUC,
and joined the Comintern, which had a Hungarian Communist,
Gerö, as its agent in Barcelona. PSUC policy in Catalonia was
directed to excluding POUM, a Marxist anti-Stalinist party, from
power. The crushing of POUM began in December 1936, with the
exclusion of its members from the *Generalitat*, and culminated in
the tragedy of the Barcelona May Days, a confused period of
fighting between POUM/CNT militias and those of the PSUC/UGT.
As the government's new centralising policy was revealed,
opposition in Barcelona in the early months of 1937 became very
vocal. Both the Barcelona anarchists and the POUM were alarmed
at the rapid growth of communist and Russian influence. They
found the abandonment of the revolution neither easy to understand
nor to accept and they were fiercely critical of what they held to be
mistakes in government policy. Tension in the city came to a head
over a government move to take control of the telephone exchange,
held by CNT militants since the beginning of the war. All
communications abroad had to be channelled through the often
capricious CNT authorities, a continuing source of embarrassment
to Valencia. The government take-over began on 3 May. By the
evening of that day most of Barcelona was on strike, with the
POUM militia preparing to fight and CNT forces looking for a
compromise. The dispute, in which 500 people died, ended on 6
May. By then, several militants were found to have 'disappeared', or

to have been executed, events which supported the widely held conviction that under the smokescreen of the May Days the Russian secret police had used this opportunity to deal with the local 'trotskyists', the POUM [50; 51; 126].

The May Days led directly to central government control over Catalonia and to the fall of the Largo Caballero regime. Faced by a Communist Party demand for the outlawing of the POUM and the arrest of its leaders, Largo Caballero stood firm. The two PCE ministers then withdrew, but Prieto and then Largo Caballero himself resigned. If Republican 'legality' meant introducing to Spain the Stalinist tactics of the show trial and the witch hunt, the UGT leader was not willing to follow the policy to so undemocratic a conclusion.

Orwell sardonically draws attention to the smartly turned out, well-armed Assault Guards sent by Valencia to suppress the Rising and compares them with his comrades on the Aragon front, with 'hardly any revolvers or pistols and not more than one bomb between five or ten men' [135, *p. 36*]. By April, he tells us, Barcelona had become a very different city. Everywhere could be seen 'officers of the Popular Army, wearing an elegant khaki uniform . . . all of them had automatic pistols strapped to their waists; we, at the front, could not get pistols for love or money' [135 *p. 107*]. The city's social aspect too had been transformed. Gone was the rough equality of dress and manners, proudly displayed. Now there were 'fat, prosperous men, elegant women, sleek cars' and 'the normal division of society into rich and poor, upper and lower class, was reasserting itself' [135 *p. 107*].

How significant were the Barcelona May Days? Did they alter the course of the war? Were they no more than a rising of *incontrolados*, of the wild men of POUM and the CNT? Or was this minor civil war within the Republican camp a result of a *putsch* by the central government and communists to bring the two major left-wing groups in Barcelona into line, with the armed reaction of POUM and CNT an unexpected consequence? Historians are deeply divided on this issue. Hugh Thomas describes the events as 'the Barcelona riots' [46 *p. 660*]. Gabriel Jackson sums up the results in these words: 'The Left militia were disarmed and military discipline was established on the Aragon front' [32 *p. 370*]. Broué and Témime argue that it 'sounded the knell of the Revolution and heralded political defeat for all and death for some of the revolutionary leaders' [51 *p. 288*]. The oral evidence gathered by Ronald Fraser [126] supports Orwell's interpretation. From a point of view sympathetic to POUM and the CNT, Noam Chomsky subjects what might be termed the Hugh Thomas/Gabriel Jackson interpretation to close analysis and textual cross reference and argues that 'there is much reason to believe that the will to fight Franco was significantly diminished, perhaps destroyed, by the policy of authoritarian centralisation undertaken by the Liberal-Communist coalition, carried through by force. "There was", observed one Italian militiaman, "no longer a war to build a new society and a new humanity" ' [100, *p. 96*].

Burnett Bolloten has traced the worsening relations between Largo Caballero, the PCE and, behind the Communists, the Soviet Union, which largely account for the successful manoeuvre which removed the Prime Minister [50]. After the fall of Málaga in February 1936, the communist press had mounted a campaign against him for failing to create a firmly disciplined Popular Army which could have prevented such disasters. Furthermore, Largo Caballero had shown himself less than receptive to some of Stalin's suggestions, particularly the proposal that the Socialist and Communist parties should be fused into one unified party (as they were in Catalonia), with the new title of Unified Socialist Party – a title which would suggest that the traditional Socialist Party existed still, but under another name, while in fact the Communists would assume a dominant role. Largo Caballero's own worsening relations with the Soviet Ambassador, and the attacks upon the Spanish leader within the communist press, had the effect of producing new alignments within the Socialist Party. Prieto particularly came to share the Communist view that new policies were needed in the armed forces which would give more power to the commissars to purge 'unreliables'. In this sense the May Days presented an opportunity for those who thought that Largo Caballero had served his purpose to ally with the Communists to overthrow him. How far Prieto was leagued with the Communists in this plot is still in dispute. Prieto saw clearly that some measure of political dependence on the Soviet Union was a function of Russian aid – an inevitable consequence of the failure of Britain and France to send military assistance. He pinned his hopes on a clearer insistence on the concept of the bourgeois republic, which was also the Russian line, as a means of convincing the Anglo-French leaders of their duty to help fellow democratic Spain. In order to enhance the respectability of the Republic in foreign eyes *prietistas*, Republicans and Communists combined to replace the working-class trade-unionist Largo Caballero with the middle-class Dr Juan Negrín. The new Prime Minister, as well as being a *prietista*, was a university professor of physiology with substantial private means, and a man whose style of life as a gourmet and womaniser was far removed from the personal austerities of the veteran UGT leader whom he replaced.

The debate over the nature of the Republican army, its discipline, its hierarchy, its punishments, its uniform and insignia, had begun with the war itself. For many Socialists and for most anarchists a people's army must in no way resemble the pre-Civil War Army, which had reflected so accurately the social structure of pre-revolutionary Spain. The Giral government had moved swiftly to deal with the problem of conflicting allegiances by relieving conscript soldiers of their military obligations and in the areas still held by the Republic working-class conscripts either went home or joined the new militia armies. Durruti's famous concept of the 'People Armed' had at last been realised and militia organisation ran all the way through the tight discipline of the Communists' Fifth Regiment to the anti-authoritarian practices of the CNT/FAI columns, organised in groups of ten, with elected leaders, roughly equivalent to NCOs, but without their powers [*Doc. 7*].

Republican virtue was no adequate defence against Franco's crack troops, however, nor was popular enthusiasm or simple courage. The speed of Franco's advance towards Madrid was an indication of the difficulties faced by militia, ill-armed, often untrained and under-equipped, in holding terrain contested by a superb fighting force. One of Largo Caballero's first tasks, therefore, when he took power as the head of the Popular Front government – even though this did not at first include the CNT – was to try to create an army to match Franco's. A week before he formed his administration, Largo Caballero made plain to Mikhail Koltzov, Stalin's representative in Spain, his antipathy towards the idea of creating a new regular army, for which both the Communists and the Soviets were pressing; instead he placed his faith in the concept of working-class militias. Once in control, however, and with Franco at the gates of Madrid, he became rapidly aware of the structural defects of the existing system of militias [50; 64]. At the end of September, therefore, he issued a decree ordering the 'militarisation' of all militia units. The old pattern of the traditional Army was to be followed in the command structure, with the promise of promotion from the ranks for able soldiers. The revolutionary nature of the army was symbolised in various ways: by the clenched fist salute, by the militia's five-pointed star as the new badge, and by the appointment of political commissars with responsibility for 'correct political thinking'. The initial formation was of twenty-one

Brigades, 1–6, XI–XV and 16–25. The XI–XV were to become the famous International Brigades, recruited from sympathisers throughout the world. Largo Caballero himself was the head of the new army, with the rank of Generalissimo, and he was advised by a general staff recruited from the left-wing parties. Russian officers took part in the tactical discussions although they had no part in the formal Committee structure.

The appointment of political commissars was no new departure. From the first days of the war, trade unions and parties had appointed commissars to keep an eye on the political reliability of regular army officers and to exercise political discipline over the men. What was new was the appointment of so many Communists to these key posts and to the general commissariat of war, entrusted with political and social oversight of the new army. Largo Caballero appointed Álvarez del Vayo commissar general and Felipe Pretel secretary general, both of whom (according to Burnett Bolloten) secretly promoted the interests of the Communist Party [50].

The CNT/FAI militia remained virtually independent of the new Popular Army and generally impervious to the control of the war ministry. The CNT position was, in the words of one observer, that 'the army is enslavement. Down with chains!', and its insistence on anarcho-syndicalist decision making, based upon consent and discussion, with its emphasis upon the ultimate need for personal liberty, made assimilation by the Popular Army extremely difficult. Until the spring of 1937 anarchist forces retained their autonomy, but the new hierarchical political organisation created in May brought them firmly within the new framework, although they preserved their own unit formation and their distinctive identity.

6 THE USE OF TERROR

In the early days of the war there was some indiscriminate shooting of enemies and potential enemies on both sides, as well as the settling of private scores [126]. Class differences were a continuing provocation, with working-class trade unionists suspected by one side, and the tie-wearing members of the bourgeoisie by the other. In this respect the very openness of Republican Spain was a disadvantage. Accounts were published abroad, relayed by consuls and others, of Popular Front atrocities or of the pillage of churches which tended only to confirm already existing prejudices about the disorderly state of Spain since the February elections. On the insurgent side, their military control and their ostentatious commitment to the ideal of a Christian Spain successfully masked the extent of their bloodily repressive measures. When the foreign press published some particularly discreditable story such as Jay Allen's dispatch describing the Badajoz massacres by Colonel Yagüe, the Nationalists were ready with some alternative account. The differences between the two sides lay not only in the extent and duration of their terror but also in the attitude of the authorities concerned. The Nationalist terror lasted throughout the war (and after) while terror in the Republican areas was at its height in the early days of the war and then declined rapidly with the reassertion of Republican legality. Again, on the Nationalist side terror and unrestricted cruelty was a matter of policy, approved and supported by the Nationalist command, while on the Republican side such tactics were officially deplored and increasingly curbed – at least until the fall of Largo Caballero, when the newly formed secret police, the SIM* and the growing war psychosis made repression more common.

In the Republican zone old scores were settled, as Gerald Brenan records of his village near Málaga [121]. In Catalonia these acts of revenge could involve whole classes, such as factory owners or priests; in Madrid it might be CEDA voters or those who, like the opposition politicians in the Model prison, were called potential traitors. What so disgraced the Republic in the early days of the war was the *paseo*,* with a car arriving at the chosen victim's home late at night, the 'arrest' and the last journey to a nearby wall where the victim was quickly dispatched [*Doc. 5*]. In Madrid and Barcelona such *paseos* were a nightly occurrence. The government finally set up popular tribunals to try to end the nightly search for victims, although militia men still took the law into their own hands.

By the winter of 1936 Republican legality was the norm, with only occasional lapses. In the Nationalist zone, however, terror was a continuing policy. Nationalist commanders were faced with the problem of maintaining control of areas with large numbers of Republican sympathisers and terror here was seen as both politically and militarily necessary in order to curb resistance movements. The Nationalists therefore concentrated their attention on potential leaders of local guerrillas. In Andalusia, for instance, this policy was followed vigorously. Nightly on Seville Radio, General Queipo de Llano promised death and mutilation to anarchist and left-wing sympathisers in the countryside around. A subsequent broadcast would confirm that his loyal Moors had carried out his threats to the letter. In such a way was Andalusian anarchism destroyed. Surprisingly, a similar policy of extirpation was carried out in the occupied Basque Provinces, an area where a more conciliatory approach might have won friends. The massacre of Republicans at Badajoz in Extremadura (both Jay Allen and Herbert Southworth cite a figure of 1,800 killed) was widely publicised at the time in the world press. Ronald Fraser's investigations at the end of the 1970s show that persecution in the villages was commonplace [126]. The involvement of the Church in such repression was documented in Majorca by the French Catholic writer, Georges Bernanos, who gave a detailed account of the arbitrary rule of an Italian Blackshirt, the self-styled Count Rossi, whose nightly murder squadrons operated in Palma and the surrounding countryside, yet who was honoured in the religious celebrations held in the island [*Doc. 6*].

In the Republic, honour was accorded to artists and intellectuals such as Casals, Lorca and Giner. In Nationalist Spain, Lorca had been an early victim of the Right in his native town of Granada, where Ian Gibson's investigations have revealed the complexities surrounding his murder [66], and in Salamanca Franco's most distinguished supporter, the philosopher Miguel de Unamuno, Rector of Salamanca University, was broken by Nationalist pressure. Unamuno stood for the 'Generation of '98', for Spain's intellectual renaissance. Initially he had supported the Rising, but he had been increasingly saddened by the turn of events in Nationalist Spain, by the death of Lorca and by the deaths of close friends in Salamanca. In the autumn of 1936, at the ceremonial opening of the new academic year, he had been angered by slurs cast upon Basques and Catalans – he himself was a Basque – and unexpectedly he rose to defend the traditional civilised values of *his* Spain. The shout of the *africanista*, General Millán Astray, 'Death to intellectuals', interrupted his speech. In public disgrace – with the implicit threat of execution hanging over him – he was dismissed from his post and died within three months. In a letter written shortly before he died, he expressed his fear that the new dictatorship would bring 'death to freedom of conscience, freedom of investigation, and the dignity of Man' [126].

The Nationalists offered an image of a new Spain, tough, military, disciplined, Catholic; a Spain where there was no place for the intellect, for separatism or even political participation. Behind that façade was the ugly reality of continuing repression and a calculated policy of judicial murder. The Republic stood publicly for a democratic Spain, for intellectual values and for dissent, for a culture which was European rather than narrowly Spanish, for discussion and for rule from below rather than control from above. The decline in the Cortes and the increasing power of the Communists was one reality behind the public stance. Another was the casual assassination after mock trials and the murder of class enemies which made the reality very different from the Republican ideal. The Republic suffered from its inability to control its supporters, particularly the more doctrinaire anarchists, but at least it made an attempt. In the Nationalist zone, on the other hand, the zealots were in power and terror was the order of the day.

7 A NEW BEGINNING – OR OLD-STYLE MILITARY AUTOCRACY?

When the Rising began, the Falange was an insignificant minority party, with its *Jefe Nacional* in prison in Alicante. In the February elections, the party had received no more than 40,000 votes, and no Falangist deputy had been elected. Yet within a year, the Falange had become the state party, indeed the only party, and, forcibly married to the Carlists, the political base for the 'New Spain' Franco had promised. Its membership had shot up to several hundred thousand, which by the end of the war had reached nearly a million. What had produced so rapid a promotion, so grand a change in its fortunes?

Initially, this phenomenal increase had come from those parts of Spain conquered by the Nationalists, with new members who, as a matter of conviction or convenience, decided that the best hope for the future, either personal or national, lay with a radical party which promised freedom from the social and political shackles of the past. In the long term, its growth was fostered by the simple fact that, not only did no other party exist, but that political, social and economic advancement depended on membership. For the victors, to be a Falangist, preferably a *camisa vieja*,* was the way to share the spoils.

As the older right-wing parties faded away, only the Carlists and the Falange remained, both of which offered a militia for active young men who wanted to fight the 'Reds', militias which were right-wing counterparts to the CNT and UGT militias in the Republican zone. The Carlists had only a limited appeal to a conservative, Catholic Spain, whereas the Falange offered to those of the Left who found themselves trapped within the Nationalist camp, at least a hope of social and economic change. However, even before Franco exploited this theme, the Falange increasingly took up the cause of Spain's great Catholic traditions, so that the original doctrine expanded to include a militant crusading Christianity.

On 20 November 1936, José Antonio, after a trial before a local magistrate, was shot in Alicante prison. The Spanish Anarchists were opposed to his execution and saw him as 'a Spanish patriot in search of solutions for his country'. The Madrid government would have commuted the sentence, but the local party bosses pre-empted its decision. What is especially significant is that General Franco did little to try to save the Falangist leader, a man who might well have been a dangerous rival, with his known ability to command liking and respect across the whole of Spain's political divide for his courage and chivalrous conduct. Honoured after his death as *el ausente*, the absent one, he was made a duke in 1947 and then given the final accolade of a burial in the Valley of the Fallen, that grandiose monument to the Francoist regime built over twenty years in the granite slopes of the Sierra de Guadarrama near Madrid.

After José Antonio's death, the Falange became subject to intrigue and faction, with Manuel Hedilla, a Santander provincial leader, emerging as the main contender for the succession. Hedilla differed vastly from José Antonio in class background. Whereas José Antonio had been a lawyer and landowner, Hedilla represented the new kind of working-class leader, rare in the Falange, a committed hard-working man who commanded a very loyal following. On 18 April 1937 Hedilla was elected *Jefe Nacional*, only to be swept away by General Franco within a matter of hours – a victim of the Nationalists' political necessity to establish some kind of political base for the Military Rising [35].

Luck, prudence, judgement – all had played their part in Franco's emergence as the omnipotent leader of Nationalist Spain. Hitler's decision to send German transport planes to Franco in Morocco, and the subsequent airlift of the Army of Africa to the mainland, had put Franco at the head of the most powerful military force in Spain. To create a skeleton political structure for the military conspirators, an interim National Defence Council had been hastily set up in July, with General Cabanellas, a veteran of 64, at its head. This had been replaced in late September when Franco was nominated not only overall military commander (Generalissimo) but also Head of State. General Sanjurjo had originally been intended for this role, but after his death the only other possible contender was General Mola, the 'Director' of the conspiracy. Franco's elevation, therefore, was a recognition of the real balance of power within the Nationalist sector. The new government's political programme was extremely vague: the Nationalists were against the 'Reds' and all they stood for, but there was little else. Serrano Súñer, an ex-CEDA deputy for Saragossa, and Franco's brother-in-law, was the *éminence grise* who proposed that Franco should become the leader of a Falange expanded by the unwanted and unwilling addition of the Carlists (the Traditionalists).

In his call for the unification of Carlists and Falangists, made in Salamanca on the night of 18 April 1937, Franco set out a highly dramatic and partisan historical interpretation to establish a political 'justification' both for this arbitrary fusion and for the 'New Spain'. The National Revolution demanded unity in service to the 'Movement' which essentially was not a fixed programme but 'flexible' and 'subject to constant revision and improvement'. His broad historical sweep began with the Reconquista, when Catholic Spain inexorably pushed back the frontiers of Moorish Spain, and the establishment of the Christian Empire of Imperial Spain. This was the first heroic phase. His second phase made politically respectable what Franco himself called the 'Carlists' struggle (in the nineteenth century) of an ideal Spain against a bastard Spain, 'a Frenchified and Europeanised Spain of the liberals', when the essential Spain had been kept alive in 'the rugged terrain of Navarre'. With great political astuteness, Franco divided the third phase into two parts: the regime of Primo de Rivera and the creation of the *Falange Española*. All these 'phases and personalities came together for the joint struggle' on 17 July, when the Rising began in North Africa. Franco's net was cast wide enough to bring in the whole of rightwing conservative and Catholic Spain, as well as Carlists and Falangists [5].

On the next day the Decree of Unification was issued, and the Falange with its comprehensive new name, the *Falange Española Tradicionalista y de las Jons,** was reborn as the state party of the Nationalist sector of Spain, with Franco as its *Jefe Nacional*. The unfortunate Hedilla, with some substantial support – including that of Pilar Primo de Rivera, José Antonio's sister – refused to serve on the new political secretariat, but was arrested and sentenced to death on a series of bizarre charges and then, with his sentence commuted, held in prison until 1941. The rebels now had a political programme – of sorts – and a developing national framework for political organisation within a totalitarian state. Increasingly, too, Falangist radicalism was quietly buried within the ferro-concrete of the Francoist state, although the Labour Charter of 1938 paid lipservice to the Falangist social programme. It promised holidays with pay and maintained stoutly that all Spaniards had the right to work, and consequently that one of the duties of the state was to maintain that right. The dynamic participatory scheme of national syndicates sketched out by José Antonio was replaced by a system of syndicates inspired by 'the principles of Unity, Totality and Hierarchy' which would be rigidly controlled by the state. The ramifications of the political and industrial structure of the New Spain promised jobs for Francoist stalwarts and a splendid scope for corruption of all kinds in the new bureaucracy. The Nationalists even failed to build on the modest agrarian reforms of the early 1930s or those promised by José Antonio, for behind the façade of their New Spain lay the old Spain, 'the domination of a class, the big landowners, the old aristocracy, the oligarchs', as Broué and Témime observe [51 *p. 459*].

In rejecting the Liberal State, Franco could claim that he was following the doctrine as proclaimed by José Antonio. Parliamentary majorities and Parliament itself, collective responsibility, elections based upon universal suffrage, free collective bargaining, the right to strike, the rule of law – all were swept away. The new state had a hardly comprehensible ideology. In the New Spain General Franco was *Caudillo** by the grace of God, not by the will of his fellow Spaniards or even as head of a political party. He was also Head of State and Head of Government, *Jefe del Movimiento** and Generalissimo of the Armed Forces. In effect he *was* Spain. The Movement had a grandiose political structure, running from a National Council down to local groups, but the Falange failed to achieve the fundamental aim of making party membership essential for senior administrative or political posts. In this respect it never resembled the German National Socialist movement in its permeation of the hierarchy or society.

Radicalism, even a limited welfare-ism, costs money, and in a country with so narrow and inequitable a tax system as that of Spain, only a positive Falangist policy adopted by the state could have carried through the fiscal and social revolution necessary to transform the Spain of the 1940s. Of that vision there was no sign in a country where the defeated half of the population was excluded and where the dominant concern was to share the spoils amongst the victors and old comrades-in-arms.

Although Francoism did not initially develop that radical social policy which might have served to create a bridge between the two Spains, what it offered instead was a special relationship with the Church. Very quickly the Nationalists began to use the concept of a crusade as a justification for the Rising. The crusade gave purpose to a movement singularly lacking in purpose and partly expressed the almost universal support that the Church gave the rebels. The ecclesiastical hierarchy publicly supported the Rising – with two distinguished exceptions, Bishop Múgica of Vitoria and Cardinal Vidal of Tarragona – and in their Collective Letter of 1 July 1937 the bishops argued that the Rising could be justified on Thomist authority as legitimate self-defence, and referred to the 'irrefutable documentary evidence' that the *alzamiento** had prevented a planned Soviet revolution in Spain. In the days immediately following the capture of Toledo, the Bishop of Salamanca had likened the Republic to the earthly city of St Augustine, in contrast to the celestial city inhabited by the Nationalists. In the same pastoral letter, the bishop had referred to the Rising as a 'crusade', conjuring up Castile's Reconquista of Moorish Spain.

The Church's support, which made abundantly clear where a Spanish Catholic's military duty lay, was amply repaid by Franco and created an informal alliance between the regime and the Church which lasted well into the 1960s, when the intellectual tide began to turn and the Church's record in the Civil War was brought under scrutiny by the Church itself. The separation of Church and State, the earliest of the Republic's reforms, was reversed. Once more clergy were paid by the state and church building subsidised. Side by side with state censorship ran ecclesiastical censorship. In all classrooms the display of the Virgin became obligatory, and in all universities, the crucifix. The Jesuits were allowed to return to Spain and all Catholic organisations enjoyed a freedom of association granted to no other group in Spain [143; 149].

The flavour of the New Spain was not heroic, not military, but fusty and ecclesiastical, a revived and impoverished mock-sixteenth-century Spain, with religion permeating every aspect of social life. Not a religion marked by compassion for all men, but a religion used to justify the immediate past and to provide a buttress for a manifestly unjust society. The New Spain was repressive of ex-Republicans, of men of the Left, of all aspects of liberal thought, a country where the policeman and priest stood on permanent guard. The Spain of the 1940s and much of the 1950s was hermetically sealed against Europe, against theatre, cinema, literature, new ideas, until in the 1960s the stealthy growth of Marxism presaged the ironic revenge that history was taking. Spain became a cultural desert in which the only true theatre was found in the Church and its great religious festivals.

8 THE MILITARY CAMPAIGNS

If the saga of Madrid can be interpreted as the victory of determined amateurs (with a professional leavening) over pure professionals, its sequel reflects in a diluted form similar virtues and similar defects. Government by committee, by party and by trade union slowly gave way to a more familiar, hierarchical system, with little, if any, pressure successfully exerted from below. The new Popular Army, however, still displayed some of its original characteristics even under its new masters. The problems were diverse. Localism and conflicting political loyalties were the most important, exacerbated by an almost universal suspicion of the communists. There were simple difficulties in communication, with Russian commanders able to give orders only in Russian, or International Brigaders speaking little or no Spanish. In the campaigns, what was most disturbing was the failure of the Republic to hold any new ground. There were major offensives, at Teruel and on the Ebro, leading to the occupation of Nationalist territory, but this was followed by its loss, at great human and material cost.

The first major defeat for the Republic was the loss of the Basque Provinces, including Bilbao, one of the two major industrial cities of Spain. The Basque Provinces, profoundly Catholic, nevertheless had opted for the Republic, mainly because of Madrid's willingness to agree to the Basque demand for autonomy. Their relationship with the Republican government was never easy and perhaps could have been severed by a skilled diplomatic initiative. Indeed, before the Nationalist attack began, the Spanish Primate, Cardinal Gomá, put to Franco the Vatican-inspired suggestion that some accommodation with the Basques might be made. Franco, as ever, was inflexible: nothing must be conceded to the enemy. The Basque campaign began in March 1937, when, leaving Madrid under siege, Franco moved the main bulk of his army to the North. The defence of the Basque Provinces presented two tough military problems for the Valencia government. In the first place, spare troops available in

Aragon or Catalonia could not be moved overland to the assistance of the Basques; the only available tactic was the use of diversionary attacks such as that upon Brunete. Again, military-political relations between the Basques and the Largo Caballero government were never easy. There had always been a Republican commander, General Llano de Encomienda, nominally responsible for the Northern front, but the reality was that his orders were virtually ignored by the local commanders. In practice, it was the Basques themselves who took decisions – a crucial factor, particularly in the closing stages of Franco's attack, when they refused to comply with the Valencia government's demand that war factories should be destroyed.

The Basque campaign demonstrated the psychological and military importance of superiority in the air. From their base in Vitoria, the Nationalists were free to strafe and bomb, without any Republican response, as the Republican command was unwilling to risk its planes by flying them over Nationalist-held territory. Their bombing campaign was launched against the small towns in the Basque Provinces, of which the most famous victim was Guernica. This attack seared itself into the world's imagination, first by the magnificent despatches of the correspondent of *The Times*, G. L. Steer [84], and then subsequently by Picasso's imaginative painting.

On Monday, 26 April 1937, the Condor Legion bombed the Basque market town continuously for three hours, beginning in the late afternoon. After first dropping heavy explosive bombs, the Germans sprayed the town with incendiaries and then machine-gunned the inhabitants as they fled. The two main military objectives, the bridge and the armaments factory, stood intact after the bombing. Undamaged, too, was the Tree of Guernica, the symbol of the ancient liberties of the Basques. The town itself was obliterated. Nothing like this had ever happened before in Western Europe and Guernica became a warning of what form any new European war might take. Why, it was asked, was this small town singled out for such exemplary treatment? The suggestion that Göring was trying out new terror tactics is untrue, since the first news he had of the raid reached him when it was already over. The most likely explanation is that the local German Air Command acted out of growing impatience with the slowness of the Nationalist advance. It seems unlikely that the Germans took their decision without at least informing their Spanish allies, although the Nationalists may not have quite taken in the enormity of the proposal. Immediately after the event, the panic-stricken Nationalist press office in Salamanca put out an alternative version: the town, it claimed, had been dynamited and then burnt by retreating militia. Franco Spain adhered to this belief until the late 1960s. The extraordinary history of this myth has now been charted by Herbert Southworth [82] [*Doc. 12*].

After Guernica, two unrelated attempts were made to bring the war to an end. On 7 May Julián Besteiro, on an official visit to London, and briefed by President Azaña, asked Anthony Eden, the British Foreign Secretary, to act as mediator. A fortnight later, the Pope floated a peace initiative, raising at the same time the suggestion that Spain's endemic social inequalities might be the basic cause of the war. Neither of these proposals got beyond Franco's stubborn refusal to contemplate any negotiated peace. He rejected out of hand any attempt to find a social, rather than a political, explanation of the war.

Did Guernica's destruction affect the subsequent course of the Northern campaign? The Nationalists, who were sensitive to world Catholic reaction to the town's fate, did not use the same tactic again, but the knowledge that they had such a weapon in reserve may have sapped Bilbao's will to resist. Another factor was the Basque government's decision to evacuate the city after the 'iron ring', the city's outer defences, had been breached. Bilbao was entered, undefended, on 10 June. Santander, the only other major town still held for the Republic, capitulated on 26 August.

What particularly disgraced Santander's surrender was Franco's treatment of the Basque notables, who had been given by their Italian captors a promise of a safe passage. Two British ships waited in the harbour to honour this pledge but, on Franco's orders, the harbour was blocked and the Basques forced to disembark. Reassured that the surrender conditions would be safeguarded, the Italians reluctantly handed over their prisoners. Trials and executions began at once.

In the moment of victory the Nationalists displayed no magnanimity or even political wisdom. The Basques had behaved with chivalry and compassion towards Franco supporters held in prison. Government officials made it a matter of personal honour to see such prisoners handed safely over to the Nationalists at the end of the campaign. No such civilised concern prompted the victors. Although there was no mass slaughter such as had disgraced the Nationalist capture of Badajoz or Málaga, the victors shot committed Republicans and even Catholic priests who had been overt supporters of the Republic. Had the Nationalists displayed political tact by allowing the Basques some cultural freedoms, they might have won over a population with which, in religious terms, they had much in common. Instead, the Basque language was suppressed and a uniform Castilian culture imposed upon the Basque Provinces.

To deflect the Francoist forces in the North, the Republic opened a series of campaigns on the Aragon front. There were two initial failures: an attack upon Huesca in May and an offensive against Segovia. Negrín then tried out the new Popular Army against Brunete, challenging Franco's control of the western approaches to the capital. The Communist-led forces of Lister and El Campesino were both involved, together with two divisions of the International Brigade, with Fred Copeman leading the British Battalion in the XVth Brigade [124]. The Republic put 80,000 men in the field against a lightly held front, but initial victory was followed by defeat when Franco brought up his reserves. The human cost was high: 42,000 casualties, of whom 25,000 were Republican. There were heavy losses amongst the Internationals, including the English writer, Julian Bell. On both sides military conduct was deplorable. 'Three hundred of El Campesino's men were surrounded', writes Hugh Thomas, 'and taken prisoner. They were all later found dead, with their legs cut off. Shortly afterwards El Campesino captured and shot four hundred Moors' [85 p. 717].

In the early months of 1937 both the Republic and the Nationalists had undergone a political crisis, resulting in fundamental political and military changes. Where the Republic was concerned, the Barcelona May Days had solved the running problem of the relationship between the revolution and the war and had tightened Communist control of the war machine. On the Nationalist side the new unification had given sole political and military control to General Franco. Both sides had completed the reorganisation of their armed forces. The Nationalists had introduced conscription, with a call-up age of eighteen. By November 1937, according to Stanley Payne, the Nationalist army numbered 600,000, about a third more than the Republicans [15]. With more tanks and more aeroplanes, the Nationalists were beginning to outclass, as well as outnumber, the Republican forces.

Negrín's policy of continuing the war was based upon his personal conviction that, given time, Britain and France would come to the aid of the Republic. As he saw the international situation, war among the European powers was inevitable, and then Republican Spain would be seen as an obvious and necessary ally of the Western democracies. On this assumption there was much to be said for a military policy of just holding on; a more adventurous policy, if it had failed, might well have opened the way to a Nationalist victory. However, General Rojo, the Republic's Chief of Staff, and Prieto, as Minister for War, were anxious to try out the newly reorganised Popular Army. The opportunity came when the Republican command had intelligence of Franco's intention to renew the attack upon Madrid, with a drive through Guadalajara. Once again, as at Brunete, the Republican strategy was designed to force Franco to move his troops to defend a lightly held front, this time at Teruel. The town was small, of about 20,000 inhabitants, and all the advantages of surprise lay with the Republican troops. In mid-December, in bitter weather, the assault began and by 8 January 1938 Teruel had been won. Franco now decided, against the advice of his advisers, to abandon the attack on Madrid in order to recapture Teruel, and by 22 February he had achieved his objective. The last stages of Franco's offensive had involved a massive aerial and artillery attack which wiped out Republican resistance. The Republican commander, General Rojo, as Raymond Carr indicates, suffered continually from the indiscipline of his troops [54]. CNT brigades mutinied and 46 soldiers were shot; and the Communist commander, El Campesino, complains bitterly in his memoirs that his fellow-Communist General Lister deserted him [123].

Victory at Teruel brought a familiar inter-allied argument over tactics. The Condor Legion commander wanted to use his motorised units in a swift dash for the coast. The gulf between the new tactics (used with such devastating effect in the German advance across France in 1940) and Franco's traditional military thinking was clear: in his view wars were won by infantry advance, not by tanks, which should have only a supporting role. A further wrangle arose over the Italian air raids on Barcelona, in which more than 1,000 people had been killed. These had been sanctioned by Mussolini, without any reference to Franco and the Spaniards. Under pressure both from the Vatican and from Great Britain, Franco intervened and they were brought to an end.

The massive scale of Franco's victory alarmed France, with Leon Blum once more in power and a short-lived Popular Front government in office. To the French Prime Minister, France's potential enemies seemed to be increasing, with Franco's victory coinciding with Hitler's advance into Austria on 11 March. Blum responded immediately, and on 17 March the French frontier was re-opened to allow arms deliveries to the Republic. Some thought, too, was given to despatching a military contingent to aid the

Republic. However, with the fall of Blum's government this moment of fellow feeling passed, and once more, on 13 June, the frontier was closed.

Teruel was the gambler's throw, which, when lost, proved to be the turning point of the war. When Franco's armies moved forward again, the momentum of the Nationalist advance carried them to the Mediterranean, to Vinaroz, north of Valencia, where they arrived on 15 April. Catalonia was now cut off from both Madrid and Valencia. From Vinaroz, Franco could turn north to Catalonia or concentrate on the reduction of Valencia. Again, in the face of all advice, he chose to attack Valencia. The Battle of the Ebro, the last great campaign of the Civil War, was the result of Negrín's and Rojo's plan to relieve pressure on Valencia by a major sweep into Nationalist territory, and Pérez López gives a graphic account of the epic crossing of the river Ebro [136]. The Nationalists, however, who had superior artillery and command of the air, within a week had held the advance. They then followed up with a series of counter-attacks and by October had regained most of the territory they had lost. Franco's strategy, however, although successful, came once more under critical scrutiny from his staff.

As an alternative, they proposed a holding operation on the Ebro while mounting a lightning attack on Barcelona. Such a plan was, for Franco, totally unacceptable. His preference was for a war of attrition, of annihilation, such as his campaign on the Ebro which had left 15,000 Republicans dead as against 6,500 of his own troops. In his terms this was victory. It had taken him four months to regain territory which the Republican army had seized in a week. Franco's slow advance eventually left him in mid-November poised to cross the Ebro into Catalonia.

Franco began the invasion of Catalonia on 23 December. As he advanced, the Republican army crumbled, with wholesale desertions and little effective resistance. Whereas Teruel had bisected Republican territory, the Ebro lost Catalonia. Barcelona fell on 26 January and was given over to a White Terror. Franco's first political act in the newly acquired territory was to extinguish Catalan autonomy. The Catalan language was banned. Henceforth Catalonia was to be an integral part of the New Spain, with Castilian as the official language.

9 INTERNATIONAL AID

To an industrially under-developed country, as Spain was in the 1930s, foreign military equipment was a necessity. If non-intervention had been a reality, a simple lack of armaments would have forced a stalemate and a negotiated settlement. However, on both sides of the political and military divide foreign assistance flowed in – not only guns and planes, but fighting men as well. Through the organisation of the International Brigades, volunteers joined the Republican forces, while the German and Italian governments sent troops and pilots to fight with the Nationalists.

The Soviet Union was the main supplier of the Republic; she set up the arrangements for recruiting the Internationals, and, through the Comintern, supervised the Brigades while they were in Spain. From Russia came the 'military advisers' who often surfaced as field commanders. Stalin passed on comment, cajolery and advice, not always acted upon, and certainly not always welcomed. Republican governments (like their Nationalist counterparts) much preferred the native product, be it soldier or military analysis. Most of the up-to-date equipment used by the Republic was Russian. Of the 1,300 aircraft bought abroad, Hugh Thomas estimates that about 1,000 were from Russia and most of the rest from France. In the key battles, at Madrid, at Guadalajara, and at Brunete, the Republic fought with the support of Russian tanks. However, the Soviet Union did not behave with largesse towards the Republic, handing out long-term credits like the Germans or Italians. All purchases had to be paid for and the cost was met by the transfer of gold from the Bank of Spain. This hard decision was forced on Largo Caballero by the Republic's desperate shortages, and his plight is vividly described in Louis Fischer's *Men and Politics* [64].

The contrast between the Republic's financial difficulties and the comparative ease with which Franco secured funds serves to illustrate yet again how the scales were tilted against the Republic.

Whereas Carlists, Alfonsists and Falangists had been funded from Mussolini in the years before the Rising, there had been no compensating Moscow gold for the PSOE, or financial assistance from other European Socialist parties. The decision to use Bank of Spain gold reserves, as Ángel Viñas stresses, was in fact taken not by the Socialist Largo Caballero but by the Liberal government of José Giral [91]. At first, before the closing of the frontier, the gold was used to buy French armaments. As the major Nationalist offensive drew near to the capital, the government moved the gold reserves to the safe haven of Cartagena, the Spanish naval base to the south of Valencia. From there, part was trans-shipped to Marseilles. The decision to send gold to the Soviet Union was taken when Soviet aid was promised and, legally, was based on the general provision made by Giral's decree. The first consignment of Russian supplies, tanks, artillery and armoured cars arrived at Cartagena in the *Konsomol*, on 15 October. This was the same day on which the Prime Minister informed the Soviet Ambassador that an initial shipment of gold reserves was on its way to Moscow.

Subsequently, much of the Bank of Spain's gold was sent to Moscow. The logic of this is clear: Soviet banks, unlike Western banks, were beyond the reach of any blocking that Western governments could exercise in line with policy decisions of the Non-Intervention Committee. From Moscow, the Republican government could use gold to purchase foreign currency as well as Soviet military supplies. Behind this decision, there was no Communist or Soviet plot [91], despite the sustained efforts of Franco's propagandists over many years to use it as additional evidence of the Red conspiracy to take over Spain.

That Republican Spain was forced to pay for her purchases abroad with the Bank of Spain's gold reserves was a matter of sheer necessity. Her ability to finance such purchases by the normal process of international trade had been seriously reduced. On paper, the Republic seemed to have an economic base which would lend itself readily to foreign exchange. In 1936, all Spain's major cities and her main manufacturing areas were within the Republican zone. However, her industry depended on imports or on raw materials such as ores or wool which lay deep within the Nationalist areas. On the other hand, the Nationalists, initially, not only seized the major food-producing areas (food in Republican Spain became increasingly scarce) but had within their control many of Spain's traditional exports: copper from the Rio Tinto mines, olives and sherry, tomatoes from the Canaries, pyrites – the major source for the production of sulphuric acid. After the summer of 1937, the great iron-ore resources of the Basque Province were available to the Nationalists. These exports were increasingly used to generate foreign exchange. Although Germany and Italy were to be the principal sources of foreign aid, a great deal came from impeccably democratic countries, parties to the Non-Intervention Agreement. Petrol came from Shell and Standard Oil, the Anglo-American oil companies; trucks from the United States arrived via Lisbon or Morocco. The Nationalists also bought a wide variety of goods from Britain and her colonies, cotton for tyres and guns, and from Malaya, tin used in the production of grenades. Robert Whealey has estimated that in a sample month – July 1938 – Franco bought one-third of his material from British soures [95]. Modern warfare depends upon the supply of petrol for motorised vehicles and much can therefore be made of the responsibility of American capitalists for Franco's ultimate victory. Yet British financial interests were also involved from the very beginning of the war. The Rio Tinto mines were British-owned and from August 1936 onwards Rio Tinto pyrites were exported to Nazi Germany, without British Government protest, thereby providing credit for Franco as well as a valuable raw material to a potential enemy of the United Kingdom. Aid to the Nationalists came mainly from Italy and Germany, with Italian aid estimated as roughly three times as much as German, a figure which did not include all the military aid in personnel and matériel which the Italian 'volunteers' provided. (The Italians behaved with great generosity towards their fellow fascists, eventually agreeing to a figure which was one-third of the original bill.) The Germans dealt with the Nationalists in a more business-like way. From the beginning of the war, two companies, one based in Morocco and the other in Berlin, handled all trade between Germany and the Nationalists, operating a barter system which therefore did not require foreign exchange. By 1938 this had become rather more sophisticated, allowing the Nationalists to buy military requirements from outside Germany through their own JNA (*Jefatura Nacional de Adquiciones* – a purchasing agency) and to pay in sterling – the pound then occupying the same position in world trade as the dollar in the post-Second-World-War world, with payment being made to Germany. From May 1938 onwards, Spain was beginning to repay her outstanding debts to Germany and Italy in sterling on a monthly basis. However, unlike the Republic, where all goods had to be paid for, almost exhausting the whole gold reserve by the end of the war, the Nationalists fought the war mainly on credit. The debt to Italy, for instance, was not repaid in full until 1967.

Dependence for arms upon the Soviet Union affected both politics and military strategy. Burnett Bolloten has analysed Largo Caballero's uneasy, prickly relations with the Russians [50]. They pushed their own military schemes, sometimes against the judgement of Largo Caballero himself, as in the famous example of the Brunete campaign, where the Prime Minister would have preferred an attack through Extremadura. The strand of Communist political commissars ran down through every level of the Popular Army, and at the top were Russian advisers who had to be conciliated, for on them depended, in the last resort, the flow of equipment. The political relations between the Republican governments, the Spanish Communist Party and the Soviet Union were highly complex. As Prime Minister, Largo Caballero resisted Soviet and PCE demands to discipline POUM. Even under Negrín, the moderate Socialist Prieto wielded considerable influence, as War Minister, right up to the defeat at Teruel. Negrín permitted the POUM trials and created the SIM in line with the policy of his communist allies. However, after Munich, even though the Soviet Union slowly abandoned belief in collective security, Negrín persisted in a policy based upon his expectations of Anglo-French intervention. Stalin's contribution to the Republic dwindled rapidly, and in November the International Brigades were withdrawn. Nevertheless, Negrín continued to believe in the inevitability of a new democratic alliance, thereby demonstrating his relative independence of Russian policy.

Foreign aid was critical for the Nationalists from the very beginning of the war, when Hitler's intervention dramatically changed their fortunes. Germany and Italy supplied aeroplanes in approximately equal numbers, and the Nationalists received, in total, as many as their opponents did from outside sources. Germany also sent professional soldiers and aviators in the Condor Legion, a mixed air and tank unit. On the ground, the most important foreign contribution was Italy's *Corpo Truppe Volontarie* (CTV), an armoured force of some 40,000 men which fought throughout most of the war, but particularly at Málaga and Guadalajara.

Foreign aid to Franco, fundamental in the winter drive into Catalonia in 1938, brought fewer rewards than either Hitler or Mussolini expected. Nationalist Spain joined Germany and Italy in the Anti-Comintern Pact (March 1939), but the new state that Franco constructed owed little to the German or Italian model.

When the long-expected European war began, and Franco had opportunity enough to repay Hitler, he was reluctant to place Spain too clearly in the Axis camp. At the apex of German power in 1940 he asked for economic assistance, and for a share of French North African territory, as the necessary conditions on which Spain would formally join Germany in the war. At the famous meeting with Hitler at Hendaye on 23 October 1940, Franco would not even agree to the passage of German troops across Spain to attack Gibraltar. Two years later his passive attitude allowed the Anglo-American forces to land in North Africa, an event which turned the tide for the Allies in the North African theatre of war. Hitler's main gains, in fact, were economic, with major concessions in Spanish mineral rights, of which the most valuable was the supply of wolfram, essential to the German armament industry. Even this reward was shortlived, however, for by 1943 Spanish wolfram was going mainly to the Allies, and by 1944 all supplies to Germany had been stopped.

Although most European governments were pro-Franco, or at best neutral, support and sympathy for the Republic was active in liberal and left-wing circles. For many people outside Spain, a simple version of events was current. The Rising was the work of the Italian Fascists or of the German Nazis, attempting to extend their power by subverting a democratic state – the obverse of the right wing theory of the communist conspiracy. Consequently, any support, in men, in money or even in passing resolutions, was a blow struck against fascism everywhere. Liberals had no clear understanding of the strength of Nationalist support in middle-class Catholic Spain, nor any knowledge of how far the Spanish revolution had transformed Republican Spain. The Spanish Civil War was often seen as the first campaign in the inevitable war against fascism, in every sense a European war, and not as the most recent example of Spain's perennial inability to establish a state with the power to maintain the loyalty of all Spaniards. One major strength of the Republic's case was that its government was the legally elected government of a democracy which was battling against a military rebellion fuelled by the two most authoritarian regimes in Western Europe.

From this sense that Spain's cause was democracy's cause - and to many of the Left the people's cause – sprang the readiness of young men of different classes and nations to serve in the defence of the Republic. Volunteers appeared in America, in England and in France, as well as amongst exiles from Germany, Italy and

Yugoslavia, and the road to Spain was charted by national Communist parties who, with the assistance and approval of Moscow, set up organisations to guide and control the new recruits. The communist-inspired organisations made certain that the International Brigades were run by communists, with political commissars to monitor the political beliefs of the volunteers. High command often went to foreign communists such as the Hungarian General Gal or the Romanian General Kléber. Communist control in the ranks brought discipline and often blind obedience to impossible orders [59]. Communist control at the top frequently resulted in the emergence of hopelessly incompetent commanders, like Gal himself, and caused too trusting a reliance upon Russian advisers who formulated military plans not always ideally suited to under-armed and under-trained men.

What the Brigades had in excess was courage and a willingness for self-sacrifice. Amongst the volunteers were ex-soldiers like Colonel Nathan, as well as representatives of intellectual England such as John Cornford, Julian Bell, Ralph Bates and Christopher Caudwell, but most of the Brigade members were ordinary working men. These were the raw soldiers who, pitted against the brilliant marksmanship of the Moors at Jarama, were mown down [128] [*Doc. 8*].

How important were the International Brigades in the Civil War? As a boost to civilian morale, the arrival of the XIth Brigade in Madrid on 8 November, marching in formation through the capital and widely taken for Russians, was of great psychological value. Yet within two days it had lost one-third of its 1,900 soldiers. The XIIth, arriving on 12 November, had 1,550 men. Hugh Thomas argues that their numbers were 'too small to have turned the day' but that 'their bravery and experience was crucial in several later battles' [85 *p. 480*]. Paul Preston urges that the role of the International Brigades in the defence of Madrid should not be exaggerated. They were, he argues, 'one component of a heroic effort which involved the whole population' [78 *p. 94*]. Raymond Carr argues that 'their role was exaggerated by the Communists "for propaganda purposes" as a defence of civilisation against barbarism' so that credit would accrue to the Soviet Union for their part in recruiting the volunteers [54 *p. 157–8*]. Ultimately, perhaps, the Brigade's true significance lay in helping to stiffen the resistance of the militia units by their own exemplary courage and steadfastness.

Their overall numbers were never large, less than 60,000, of whom the French, with 10,000 volunteers, were the biggest contingent; the Americans had 2,800, and the British, 2000. The

Brigades were organised into seven units, of which the XVth, the Lincoln-Washington Brigade, held most of the British and Americans. The Internationals fought in all the major campaigns of the war: at Jarama, Brunete, Belchite, Teruel and the Ebro. Nearly 10,000 died and more than 7,600 were wounded. By October 1938 there were less than 13,000 left in Spain. They went home in November 1938, a time when the war seemed as good as lost. Soviet supplies were drying up while the Nationalists were still receiving fresh German armaments. The signing of the Munich Agreement on 29 September had ended any hope that the Western democracies would support the Spanish Republic against a common foe. The humanly costly Battle of the Ebro had destroyed the Popular Army. With all the military and political cards stacked against the Republic, a negotiated peace was the only alternative to the continuance of this calamitous war. The withdrawal of the Brigaders was a move by the Spanish government to try to make a negotiated peace possible.

The Anglo-American Brigaders left behind a mass of personal accounts [124; 128; 138; 141] which have helped to establish their public as middle-class intellectuals. In fact, for the most part the Brigaders came from south Wales, Glasgow and Liverpool, from the Bronx and the New York waterfront, many of whom were members of the Communist Party.

The presence of the Brigades did much to convince the Spanish people that the outside world was genuinely concerned with the fate of Spanish democracy. In Madrid, while the Spanish government was fleeing the city, volunteers from abroad were flooding in to man the defences of the capital. Their exploits were written up by visiting newspapermen, by Ernest Hemingway, H. L. Matthews, Sefton Delmer and Martha Gellhorn. The gifted writers in their ranks gave them an international fame [83; 94]; visitors to Spain came to talk to them – C. R. Attlee and Stephen Spender from Britain and John dos Passos from America. The Brigades were seen by their supporters as the liberal conscience in action, but from the standpoint of General Franco they were the 'shock troops of international communism', carrying on a war which otherwise might well have been brought to a quick and victorious conclusion. Brigaders who fell into Nationalist hands had short shrift and Peter Kemp describes how he was forced to execute a fellow Irishman [130] [*Doc. 9*]. On the Republican side Pérez López, attached to the XVth Brigade, gives the obverse of this: the summary execution of all Italians who were taken prisoner [136].

With the reduction in popular initiative and the necessary centralisation of control under Largo Caballero and subsequently under Negrín, the International Brigades were brought within the official Spanish Army, taking the place traditionally held by the Foreign Legion. Military discipline was tightened and Spanish officers appeared side by side with French, German, English, Irish and American. In a multilingual force the problems of communication were always great, and although Internationals were called on to learn Spanish, little provision was made for them to do so. The problem of language was compounded by international rivalries, in microcosm between the British and Irish contingents, and, on a large scale, between the French and German communists. Some communist Brigade leaders were repressive and tyrannical, such as the French communist, André Marty. 'Only Stalin himself', observes Hugh Thomas, 'had a more suspicious nature than André Marty' [85 p. 458].

In the post-Largo Caballero era, control by political commissars was replaced with surveillance by the ferocious SIM. No recourse to embassies or consulates could save Brigaders from its arbitrary justice, for Brigaders had no international standing. They were in Spain without permission and their governments were unwilling to offer them any assistance. When they first volunteered they gave no thought to the need for an escape route home, and when they became disillusioned or simply reluctant to go on fighting in someone else's war, no matter how just, they had no easy way back. If they simply deserted they were likely to be caught, and even if they reached their consulate (in the case of Brigaders who were not stateless) they could be arrested before they entered the consul's office. For the Brigaders, then, there was no way out, little pay, no comforts, no well-organised system of medical relief. They came, they saw, and they left behind in Republican Spain a vision of an international community which believed in the Republic. In fact this was a mirage without substance, for France was largely quiescent, British rulers were anxious for the Nationalists to win and Americans were selling oil to Franco on long-term credits given by Texas Oil.

10 THE REPUBLIC UNDER NEGRÍN

In his analysis of the rise of the Communist Party in Spain and of the growth of Soviet influence, Burnett Bolloten sees Negrín as the tool of the Communists and the Soviet Union [50], a view which neglects Negrín's own character and his fundamental concern to maintain the Republic and to defend Spanish interests. There are, it is true, areas in which Negrín's policy seemed to have a Russian flavour. His emphasis on 'concentration', on forced unity, and in particular his attack upon the POUM seemed to echo treatment of Trotskyists in the Soviet Union. But any comparison between Negrín's Spain and Stalin's Russia reveals only a similarity of aims, not of tactics; nowhere did Spain show the degree of paranoia which marked Russian communism, with its continuing judicial murder of leading Bolsheviks and others. In Spain there were relatively few examples of this attitude. Andrés Nin, the POUM leader, disappeared into an NKVD prison in Spain, and his colleagues were brought to a show trial, charged with slandering a friendly country (the Soviet Union) and sentenced to fifteen years' imprisonment. To deal with political dissidents, Negrín established the *Servicio de Investigación Militar* (SIM),* a political police force, which grew to 6,000 agents, and established its own prisons and camps. Yet there was no indiscriminate persecution. Largo Caballero, for instance, lived on, albeit neglected, as did Prieto, after his resignation, and although there were occasional press campaigns against them, their lives were not in danger – as they most certainly would have been if Spain had simply been an Iberian version of the Soviet Union.

The Largo Caballero government had recognised the need to establish firm control of the Spanish tendency to cantonalism; Negrín carried this much further. Potential opposition papers such as *Claridad* and *Adelante* (of Valencia), hitherto run by supporters of Largo Caballero, were transferred to *prietistas*. The Cortes declined in importance and, already reduced in numbers by the withdrawal of right-wing deputies, shrank even further from 200 in October 1937 to a mere 62 in February 1939. It met only once every six months and was no more than a rubber stamp. When the Cortes met in October 1937, it was without Largo Caballero, and with none of the anarchist leaders. One other major prop of the Republic was also collapsing: the partnership with Catalonia on which the 1931 Republic had been built. Negrín took over control of the Catalan customs, and dispersed the Catalan police throughout Republican Spain. In October 1937 when Negrín moved the government from Valencia to Barcelona, he deliberately ignored the Catalans and acted without even the pretence of consultation.

It is arguable that the early experience of Republican governments had sufficiently alerted the Negrín administration to the political dangers of too much discussion, or too much devolution in decision-making, and that Negrín was developing (albeit in a tougher way) the policy begun by Largo Caballero. Under Negrín the Spanish capacity for the fragmentation of authority was finally overcome, and in the increasingly desperate military situation no other policy was perhaps possible. Chomsky's pro-anarchist argument [100], despite its brilliance, ignores the multiplication of separate activities, the wasteful frittering away of the national effort, in the Spanish Revolution. Had there been less rule from below, Catalonia's war effort might well have been more successful. Yet the supersession of all the infinite varieties of Spanish political life by a single orthodoxy had reduced the clear differences between the two opposing regimes and had most certainly weakened the Republican will to resist.

The political base of the Negrín government steadily narrowed, particularly with the resignation of Prieto in April 1938. After Teruel, Prieto had become increasingly convinced that the Republic could no longer win the war. He was attacked for defeatism in *Frente Rojo* and in Negrín's paper, *La Vanguardia*. He was offered alternative posts to the War Ministry but despite the pleas of the CNT – who wanted him to stay in order to prevent domination by the Spanish Communists – he resigned. Later he was to claim that he had grown weary of the communists – although up to Teruel he had been in full agreement with their policies. He spent the rest of the war in a vain search for a just peace. In Raymond Carr's view 'Communist pressure, ruthlessly exerted, secured his dismissal' [54]. Hugh Thomas, on the contrary, argues that 'the only explanation of this crisis is that Negrín, without communist encouragement, had determined to move Prieto from the ministry of national defence because of his defeatism' [*85 p. 813*]. All that can be said for certain is that after the failure of the Teruel offensive it is hardly surprising that Prieto should have felt that the Republic had few options left and that a negotiated settlement held the best hope for the future.

Negrín's belief, continuously expressed to his supporters, was that it could only be a matter of time before the Western democracies abandoned their ill-starred policy of appeasement, and that when this happened the Spanish Republic would benefit immediately and be brought within the perimeters of Western defence. That hope was finally dashed on 29 September 1938, the day the Munich Agreement was signed and Anglo-French appeasement policies reached their trough. On the Ebro, the Republican army was still holding fast. Immediately afterwards, Negrín spoke on Spanish radio of the need for mutual understanding, implicitly proposing peace by agreement.

The turning point in Anglo-French policy came finally on 31 March, the date of the guarantee to Poland – ironically the same day as that which had been fixed for the surrender of the residual Republican armies to the victorious Nationalists in Spain. In retrospect, however, it seems likely that even if the Republic had still been fighting, no change in Anglo-French policies would have occurred. Help might have been forthcoming at the time of the German offensive in spring 1940, but the Republic could not possibly have held out until then.

Even after the fall of Barcelona, Negrín tried to fight on. On 16 February he held a conference with his military commanders at Los Llanos airport (near Albacete) to sound out opinion. Almost without exception, they told him that Spain must have peace. The tragedy for Spain is that no honourable peace terms were ever on offer. Through Lord Halifax, Negrín offered a Republican surrender in exchange for a guarantee against political reprisals and a promise to allow all who wished to do so to leave Spain. In Madrid, Colonel Casado offered to overthrow Negrín and the Communists in return for a similar guarantee, an offer which Franco's agents accepted. The Casado coup began on 5 March, a conspiracy which reflected not only the desperation of starving Madrid but also the Casadist conviction that Negrín was working solely for the Russians. Within a week the city had been won by the Casadists, and came under the control of a National Council headed by General Miaja, with the distinguished Socialist Besteiro as Foreign Minister [55].

With Madrid under the new Junta's control, the Casadists began to try to establish a basis for an honourable surrender. But Franco would settle for nothing less than unconditional capitulation. When negotiations dragged on, he ordered an attack upon Madrid, which began on 26 March. Two days later the formal surrender of the capital took place in the ruined Hospital Clínico, in the once splendid University City. All the Junta, as well as the members of Negrín's deposed government, went into exile – except Besteiro, who stayed with his countrymen and, like so many others, died in Franco's gaols.

On 30 March the Nationalist Army entered Madrid and by 1 April General Franco controlled the whole of Spain. After the brief interlude of the Second Republic, a new era of dictatorship had begun, destined to last, albeit in an increasingly diluted form, until Franco's death in 1975.

11 RETROSPECT

The simple issue of democracy versus fascism which, in the 1930s, the Spanish struggle seemed to display, has long since faded and died. The questions which are now asked about the Civil War increasingly turn on the extent of communist influence within the Spanish Republic. The sense that this was the Last Great Cause – so vividly expressed by Jimmy Porter in John Osborne's play *Look Back in Anger* – has been replaced by a probing of the changes, political and social, which transformed Republican Spain during the war. Anarchist writers have expressed their urgent conviction that the revolution was betrayed, without ever asking what the alternatives were for the Republican government; liberal historians have deplored the growth of Soviet power in Spain, without linking this to the failure of the liberal democracies to provide arms for the Republic. The shift of interest in the studies of the Civil War helps to obscure two central issues – that the Republican government was a liberal government elected in a constitutional way and challenged by a military rising; and that the regime that took over Spain was based upon repression and continued in repression for many years to come. No reassessment of the Civil War should overlook either the nature of the pre-war government or the squalid brutality of the post-war regime [48].

In assessing war guilt, Franco's punitive Law of Political Responsibilities went back to 1934, a key year in the history of the Republic. The 1934 Asturian Insurrection did not take place in a political vacuum but within a Europe which had seen Hitler, Mussolini and Dollfuss destroy democratic regimes and within a Spain which had seemed threatened by CEDA's call for a 'new state'. The implications of 1934 ran far. On the Left, the message of the Asturias could be read as a victory for the Asturian miners in that they frustrated Gil Robles's attempted seizure of power. For the militant Left, this was the first step on the road to socialism in Spain, and they assumed that the process would be continued by further coups. Prieto, on the other hand, argued that the future for Spanish socialism lay in working within the constitutional context. Certainly, the nature of the repression in the Asturias, when the government permitted the Army to treat its own citizens as if they belonged to an enemy country, inflamed class hatreds in Spain. These disastrous class-based politics stiffened attitudes after 1934, particularly when the conservative government penalised so many different groups and held so many Spaniards in prison.

When the Military Rising began in 1936, the claim that this was intended to prevent a communist conspiracy was made more credible because of the 1934 Insurrection. Socialist unwillingness to join the coalition government, and the intransigence and revolutionism of Largo Caballero, added strength to the claim. That no such conspiracy existed is now clear. Nor was there any evidence on which the officers based their statement. The Military Rising was not a 'Generals' rising' for in the main the Generals remained loyal to the Republic. Support for the Rising came rather from the young, ultra-patriotic junior officers, who were committed to a narrow view of the kind of Spain they wanted. Their action evoked no mass support, no 'movement' of the population, except amongst the Navarrese. The great surge of support came in the large towns, and was for the Republic. From the beginning, the Nationalists were forced to cow the population into submission by recourse to execution and imprisonment.

Ironically, the Army revolt triggered off a social and political revolution, for in Barcelona, in Málaga, in Valencia and in Madrid, workers' committees based upon trade unions and political parties took over many of the functions of government. In Barcelona, for instance, the fully-fledged workers' state described by George Orwell came into being. The Republican government's reluctant decision to arm these workers' committees fulfilled Durruti's dream of 'the people armed' and made inevitable a prolonged and desperate struggle. Once this step had been taken, the continuing problem for the Republic was to create a new legal framework which would absorb the militias, undermine the voluntarism which permeated their activities, and subordinate them to military discipline – which was essential if the war was to be won. The militia armies, denied arms by the democratic countries, were forced into dependence on the Soviet Union. What is remarkable is that such military dependence did not produce in the Republic Soviet-style governments under pallid democratic forms.

In July 1936, to any foreign observer it might at a cursory

inspection seem that the political and military balance tilted firmly towards the Republic. Industrial Spain was Republican; the large cities remained loyal. However, of the forces of the state, most of the Army and the Civil Guard had deserted to the Rising – the only major exception was in Barcelona, where the Civil Guards' loyalty helped to defeat General Goded's invasion from Majorca. Again, Hitler's prompt response to Franco's call for help provided the transport planes so crucial in bringing the Army of Africa to the mainland. In the summer of 1936, the Republic had all the trappings of state authority but little real power: no army or police force to enforce its decisions. Initially, too, its authority was weakened by government indecision, hesitating between seeking a negotiated peace and arming the populace. The replacement in Catalonia and Aragon of the institutions of the state by revolutionary committees was a further source of weakness, giving propaganda fodder to the Republic's enemies and creating a continuing tension between government and its local rivals.

In any comparison between the Republic and the Francoists, the fundamental contrast must be between unity and diversity. This critical difference may be exhibited in many different ways. The Republic's clear industrial advantage has to be set against the political and social diversity of the two main industrial areas: the Basque Provinces and Catalonia. The first was conservative and Catholic, and committed to the Republic mainly because of the Madrid government's willingness to agree to devolution. Catalonia, on the other hand, was governed by a series of committees, and there was little common ground between government and province. 'Dual Power', two quite separate and radically different forms of government, continued to exist until the 1937 May Days. In Barcelona, the writ of the central government hardly ran at all.

In Franco's Spain, no dissent was tolerated. Liberal and left-wing parties were suppressed and the right-wing parties forcibly merged, creating a unified political structure with Franco at its head. Luck, too, was on Franco's side: the accidental deaths of Sanjurjo (the destined Leader) and of Mola, Hitler's preference for Franco over his rivals, the execution of José Antonio – such strokes of good fortune opened to Franco the way to supreme political and military power.

The political unification which Franco achieved, and his identification with the ideologies of the major fascist powers, meant that he had no need to find backers. Germany and Italy were only too willing to come to the assistance of a leader who seemed to share their common aspirations. No such easy identification was possible for the Republic, which was at once both democratic and revolutionary, depending on where it was inspected. The Western Powers, particularly the British, were unwilling or unable to recognise the Republic as a fellow democracy, or even as a state struggling to return to democratic norms, and were by turn either quiescent or pro-Franco. The fruitless search for friends – and at the same time the necessity of maintaining good relations with their arms supplier, the Soviet Union – led the Republican government to try to seek political unity by suppressing revolution, by creating a centralised and legal state. This policy ended the debate over which should have primacy, the war or revolution, but by destroying revolutionary élan, denied the Republic much of its ideological base.

At the level of military organisation, until the formation of the Popular Army the Republic depended upon volunteers, whereas the insurgents had a well-trained, well-armed professional force, under one command, which early in the conflict was expanded by an army conscripted from the occupied areas. The military command in the Republic was disastrously complex: in Madrid it was run by a Junta; on the Aragon front and in Catalonia by committees of POUM and the CNT; the Basque Provinces had their own command which paid scant heed to the Republican government. Again, in Catalonia, the workers' militias elected their own officers, whereas the International Brigades were largely under the control of the PCE. After October 1936, the government set out to create a united force, the Popular Army, at first with military leaders from the ranks, such as Enrique Lister, a former quarryman, or Juan Modesto, an ex-woodcutter – men whose abilities were released by the war. The problem of diversity which arose from the breakdown of the established order continued to dog the Republic, and in Raymond Carr's judgement 'the Popular Army never completely overcame the weakness of the militia system, the primacy of politics over war' and its fundamental failing was 'the independence of the various fronts and militia groups which was never absorbed into the *mando único*, the central command' [54 *p. 134*].

This lack of central command was reflected in the military strategy with which the Republic fought the war. Victors of in-fighting within political groups or between rival military commands often decided the course the campaign took. Differences between Largo Caballero and the Communists prevented the launching of an Extremadura offensive to separate Andalusia from the rest of Nationalist Spain. Political antagonisms affected Belchite, Brunete and Teruel, although, as Paul Preston maintains, at Brunete, and particularly at Teruel, new German equipment was finally crucial in deciding the issue [78]. In contrast, Franco, once he had achieved full command, brooked no opposition and allowed no criticism of his plans. His strategy was based on a determination to allow no Nationalist territory to fall into Republican hands: at all costs it must be won back. 'Dogged, uninspired and the despair of his German allies, he would sacrifice lives in unnecessary campaigns to gain militarily unimportant territory' [78]. Out-dated his military thinking quite clearly was, dominated by his success as an *africanista*, unaffected by his German advisers who sought a war of movement; yet nevertheless, the sheer size of his conscript army and the weight of technical superiority finally decided the outcome of the war.

Within Republican Spain, communist influence was reflected in the system of political commissars, and within the International Brigades, the rigorous party line, which it was unwise, often dangerous, to dissent from. It is perhaps ironic that overall Russian policy and communist influence were directed to turning back the revolutionary clock to make Spain once more a liberal democracy so as to win the good opinions of foreign observers. The communists were committed also to creating a unified political and military structure so as to end the weaknesses of hostile political factions. On the Nationalist side, unity was achieved in the new political structure imposed in April 1937, based upon the enlarged Falangist party, which gave a misleadingly fascist air to what was basically a military autocracy. Here again, the Spanish capacity to resist foreign influences was clearly displayed, for Franco and the Nationalists showed themselves continuously resistant to the policy nudges from German representatives.

In the role assigned to women, however, Nationalist Spain superficially seemed to ape her fascist and Nazi counterparts. The regimes in Germany and Italy had both tried to restrict women's role to family and kitchen, and similarly in the New Spain women were once more to be restored to their true place in society – namely, subordination to the male. Army, government and business were to remain male preserves. As in Germany and Italy, fecundity was the prime feminine virtue. For a brief moment during the war, women had been encouraged to work outside the home in armament factories, and middle-class women in particular had found useful work in the *Auxilio Social*, a Falangist charitable association modelled on the Nazi Winter Aid, which took care of the orphans and the needy. The end of the war reduced the scope for women's work, and the Falange then sought to return women to the home, stressing the loss of femininity which involvement in a man's world must necessarily bring [*Doc. 13*]. Where Falangism differed profoundly from other fascist states was in the puritanical religiosity which it displayed in offering guidance to women. Whereas Germany and Italy had women's movements independent of the Church, secular, uniformed, assertively nationalist, National Syndicalism never put down such roots. It remained a façade, and depended on the Catholic Church to regulate the role of women and to create models for the ideal Spanish woman, who should be modest, graceful, uncompetitive, seeing her life only in terms of marriage and childbearing. Religious indoctrination became the basis of female education, and a devout, dedicated and deferential role the ideal female model.

Perhaps the true Spanish tragedy is that the war went on for so long, killed so many people, did so much damage, and left behind such bitterness. After Teruel, peace seemed essential. But no peace was on offer, except unconditional surrender. There was no promise of reconciliation, only a promise of retribution; no call to join in the building of a new and peaceful Spain, only a fearful certainty that for the defeated Franco's Spain offered no refuge. For many Spaniards, death or exile were the only choices. It is fair to say that Franco behaved honourably in not making facile promises. What cannot be said is that he acted wisely, for the legacy left by the Civil War was to divide Spain until the 1980s.

12 THE LEGACY OF THE CIVIL WAR

SPAIN AND THE WORLD OUTSIDE

Only very rarely in modern history had Spain been brought into contact with her European neighbours. The last occasion had been in the Napoleonic wars, when some of the major battles of the British campaign against France were fought on Spanish earth. After 1815, Spain withdrew once more behind her natural and cultural frontiers, the object of European investment and marginal political involvement by the great powers, only to be dragged bloodily into Europe again by the Military Rising. Then, quite suddenly, Europe rediscovered Spain and European political rivalries were again fought out on Spanish territory. When the Civil War was over, Spain withdrew from Europe for a further decade, trying to recover from the desolation the struggle had created. The Spanish war, at the cost of great suffering for the Spanish people, allowed Europe to see a preview of the new tactics and equipment that would be the hallmarks of a major European war. Without German aeroplanes – first transport, and then fighters and bombers – or even without Soviet fighters and tanks, the war would have been very different and far less devastating. The use of bombers against undefended towns; the continuous shelling of civilian populations, the deployment of troops with air cover – these and many other aspects of the Spanish Civil War provided valuable military lessons for the major European powers, but not for Spain herself. All that she gained from the inflow of foreign troops and equipment was physical devastation and the stunting of her economic growth.

Not only did Spain, in this brutal way, once more take her place in Europe – which the Right had long wanted – but she was also committed to the side of the dictators. Before Franco, Spain had been on the periphery, an object for European investment in copper, in sulphur and in railways, and if not politically committed to the Anglo-French Entente, at least not actively hostile. The Nationalist victory linked Spain in the Anti-Comintern Pact with Germany and with Italy, a political relationship backed up by a series of agreements, signed in 1938, which gave Germany privileged access to minerals needed to feed her armament industry. For Britain, the non-intervention policy which she had initiated (and almost alone adhered to) had helped to create a political threat to Gibraltar and to British control of the Mediterranean. France, too, was now in a far worse strategic position, with Francoist Spain linked so firmly to Nazi Germany.

That these implicit dangers to Britain and France did not bring disaster in the Second World War owed something to Franco's deliberate 'prudence' and a great deal to the weakness of Spain as well as the changing fortunes of the war itself. Spain was a very fragile link in the New Europe that Hitler was trying to build, a country gravely impoverished, held together by stern repression, with her population reduced by imprisonment, exile and death. Not until Hitler attacked Russia in 1941 did Franco take a positive step by sending the volunteer *División Azul** to fight with the Wehrmacht on the Russian front. After the German defeats at El Alamein (1942) and Stalingrad (1943), Franco drew back, concerned for Spain's future in a Europe which was now increasingly likely to be dominated by the Allies. He began to reface his regime, and to make overtures to Britain and America. The *División Azul* was withdrawn and Franco cautiously began to change direction.

The end of the war brought no succour to Franco – or to his opponents. Spanish Republicans in exile expected that the Allies would now turn their attention to Franco. The *Caudillo* hoped that his new, pro-Western policies would win friends. The Allies – Britain, France and the USA – contented themselves in 1946 with the publicly expressed hope that the regime would transform itself peacefully. From that point onwards the international position of the regime began to deteriorate. In December of the same year, the United Nations called for the withdrawal of the ambassadors of member states from Madrid and for new economic sanctions to be applied against Spain. Excluded from the Marshall Plan and the generous American assistance given towards the rebuilding of Europe, Spain suffered terrible years of deprivation, with near-famine conditions and industry less productive than it had been in 1918. Franco was saved once again by the wind of change produced by a shift in the international situation. With American policy becoming more and more bitterly anti-Soviet, Franco could claim an impeccable record of anti-communism. The Korean War in 1950 (seen by the USA as clear evidence of the international communist conspiracy) hardened President Truman's resolve and in August 1950 America made the first step towards bringing Spain back into the comity of nations by making her a loan of 62 million dollars.

From that initial step almost all else followed. In November the UN cancelled her 1946 resolution and Spain was permitted to join the Food and Agriculture Organisation. In 1951 the American Ambassador returned to Madrid and in 1953 the USA and Spain signed the Pact of Madrid which gave economic and military aid to Spain, in return for a mutual defence agreement. Europe, unlike America, was slower to forget and to forgive – an ironic situation in view of the general lack of support given by the European powers to Franco's opponents in Spain – and not until the death of Franco in 1975 was Spain's wish to become a member of the EEC seriously considered. Long before that, however, European conglomerates such as Renault, Fiat and Citroen had built up their Spanish ancillaries and European tourists had discovered the delights of Spanish beaches and Spanish wine. Although, in economic and in human terms, Spain had long been reintegrated into Europe, her full acceptance had to wait until her political institutions had lost entirely the authoritarian stamp imprinted by Franco and Francoism.

THE EFFECTS ON SPAIN

By the 1980s the last great cultural and political frontiers erected by the Civil War had been rolled back [144]. Men such as Manuel Cortes came out of hiding, after thirty years living hidden away by their families from the revenge of the victors [125]. The last Falangist symbols had disappeared even from the most remote mountain villages. Catalan and Basque are now once more taking their rightful place amongst the languages of the peninsula. Spaniards constantly look back to the 1930s and pore over the great mass of historical material which is flooding out of the presses. There is general agreement that it must never happen again, and Spaniards are zealously trying to find out why it ever happened at all. Supporters of the dismantled regime fight in general elections to win seats in the new democratic Cortes. Francoists still occupy high places in the Army and even in government, but they are constrained to wear a democratic face.

At the end of the Civil War nearly half a million Spaniards went into exile; most of them settled in France, but there were other groups scattered throughout the world, in Mexico, in Argentina, in England, and in the Soviet Union. Some, like the Catalan leader, Luis Companys, were handed back to Franco's vengeance by Vichy France; some were deported as labourers to Germany, some fought and died with the French Resistance. Of the great ones, many were dead – Azaña, Prieto, Largo Caballero – but those who remained began to return, amongst them Dolores Ibarruri, Salvador Madariaga and Federica Montseny. Picasso's 'Guernica', in exile on the painter's orders until the death of Franco, is now in Spain.

That the whole process was so slow was due to a very great extent to the obduracy of one man, and to the ruthlessness of the policies he fostered. Of these, the initial repression set the tone for the future. Franco's policy was one of *limpieza*, cleaning up, removing by death any opponents. The Law of Political Responsibilities (1939) made all supporters of the Republic liable to the penalties of death, imprisonment or loss of employment. To have been a Republican officer normally meant certain death, as did political commitment to one of the Popular Front parties. All over Spain the shootings went on; special camps were built to take the 'guilty' and a darkness descended over the land. In no way did Franco try to win over the defeated – they were, if not literally at least metaphorically, put to the sword as though they belonged to a different order of mankind. In the early years of the regime there were no legal norms. Military tribunals, unspecified charges, secret police, wholesale executions were the only norms by which the new state operated. Repression was the means used to prevent the rise of a future opposition. The Catalan and Basque languages were banned; trade unions, apart from the state-controlled syndicates, were prohibited; and strikes were repressed with the use of troops. The security forces hounded down suspects and those elements which were still carrying on resistance to the Nationalist regime [136].

Membership of the new state party was automatic for all existing members of the Falange, for Carlists and for all army officers. The Law of Political Responsibilities, on the other hand, laid down firmly that the defeated were to have no part in Spain's future. For those who survived and had been 'responsible' – who had, in other words, opposed the Nationalists at any time since 1934 – exclusion from any official post or from any firm having dealings with any official organisation (in effect most of Spain's commercial and industrial organisations) was the penalty. 'To the victor the spoils' was true even at the most elemental level: under Franco the Republican war-disabled were given no state pension.

For Spain the outbreak of the Second World War simply added a further dimension to her national tragedy. During the Civil War her economy had declined – compared with 1935, income per head in 1939 was 28 per cent lower. Cut off from her natural markets during the Second World War, Spain, like other countries, established a series of often bizarre economic controls, which were sometimes no more than a means to provide employment for Nationalist supporters. Her difficulties were exacerbated by a series of droughts, which Ronald Fraser has charted [7]. While other Europeans were killing each other, Spaniards were starving, saved only in 1946 by General Perón of Argentina who came to Spain's assistance with loans and credit which brought food to her people. For Franco's Spain, unlike Hitler's Germany, there were no good years to look back to. Ironically, the good years were to come with the decline of authoritarian Francoism, after the 1964 Economic Plan, with the rise of mass tourism, the growth of the construction and hotel industries, the exodus of Spanish workers abroad, a developing economic liberalism, and the slow lifting of police repression, at least in so far as it affected the population as a whole.

Yet although the Army and the Church were the victors in the Civil War, nothing is for ever. The major posts were initially held by comrades-in-arms and the Church resumed its fundamental control of much of Spanish life – the era of 'national catholicism' – but increasingly Franco came to depend upon what Kenneth Medhurst calls 'coalition management' [149] and Raymond Carr and Juan Pablo Fusi 'political chemistry' [144]. Franco held the political balance between the various groupings or 'families' which administered Spain during his rule. Francoism was never a steady state but in every sense a movement with different factions in power during its forty years of history. Initially, the regime depended upon the institutionalised 'families', the Army, the Church, the Falange (increasingly deradicalised by its new name, the 'Movement'). After 1943, when Germany and Italy were emerging as possible losers in the war, Falangists came to play an even smaller part in government and the political families rather more. Of these families, the principal one was that of Franco's comrades-in-arms; the second consisted of the monarchists (increasingly important after 1947 when Franco declared Spain a kingdom); and the third of the technocrats and the professionals who emerged with the economic 'miracles' of the 1960s.

During the 1940s the regime, finely tuned to the international situation, dropped some of the Falangist trappings, and a new concept of organic democracy, with an embryonic Cortes, and with a guarantee of human rights and the reappearance of the legal norms, began to oust the Falangist structure and rhetoric. Spain became more and more an autocracy of the pre-1931 vintage, shifting and swaying in the European winds, with the Generalissimo in the Cold War era expecting to be welcomed back into Europe as an early example of an anti-communist. That this proved to be a miscalculation did not bring a reversal to a more repressive regime and the rise of a consumer society in the 1960s pushed Spain more and more towards a rough-and-ready approximation to other European societies.

In 1952 Benjamin Welles painted a picture of the Church as a major and quiescent partner in the new state [156]. But already a new generation of priests was appearing which came to reject the whole concept of the Civil War as a crusade. HOAC*, the workers' association of the Spanish Catholic Church, became increasingly critical and left in tone, as Norman Cooper's essay shows [152], and slowly the Church began to disembarrass itself of Franco's political legacy. By 1980 the Spanish Church belonged quite clearly to the new forward-looking Church founded by Pope John XXIII, with its younger clergymen in the vanguard on almost every social question. In the Basque Provinces the Church identified itself with resistance to Franco and Basque priests were frequently to be found in Franco's jails.

The Church's interest in social questions and involvement in working-class life may partly be seen as an attempt to prevent the domination of Spain by Marxism, either through the Communist Party or the Socialist Party. The Church's apprehensions were justified to the extent that the workers' commissions and the trade unions (which were underground organisations in the 1960s but were officially recognised after Franco's death in 1975), were largely run by communists [147]. Old names like the UGT have reappeared and there is a new range of working-class parties, demonstrating the infinite Spanish capacity for individualism, with its resulting splinter groups. The industrial revolution in Spain since the mid-1960s has transformed the country socially and politically. It is an irony of history that this social and economic revolution has once more set up a liberal state, a completely updated version of the Republic of 1931, but one that retains the monarchy and is marked by a wise and mature acceptance of the diversities which underpin all modern societies, and particularly Spain.

Some characteristics of pre-Civil War Spain have largely

disappeared, fortunately amongst them the hold of anarchism on the political life of the working class. Others, after the stifling centralism of the Francoist era, have reappeared with renewed force. Regionalism and localism have developed a fierce strength, not only in the Basque Provinces which suffered so grievously from the intractability of the Nationalist regime, and in Catalonia, where Catalanism is more widely entrenched throughout the social range than ever before, but also in Andalusia, and even in Galicia and in Castile [30; 152].

Agrarian reform ended with the Civil War and land was returned to its original owners. The problem of the workless day labourer remained and of an agriculture largely unaffected by mechanisation or improvement. In the South the building boom of the 1950s uprooted agrarian labourers and turned them into building workers, and the Mediterranean coast steadily began to draw labour from the Andalusian villages [7]. State enterprise began to intervene with the creation of the INC (*Instituto Nacional de Colonización*), which took a hand in land settlement and in irrigation. By 1953 the state had initiated a land policy committed to concentrating the *minifundista** holdings. In the 1950s, also, the INV (*Instituto Nacional de la Vivienda*) developed low-cost housing and in 1957 a Ministry of Housing was established charged with supervising construction. Social security followed, and by 1966 Spain had a comprehensive welfare system. It was not the Falange but the new capitalism which brought to Spain a system of social provision not markedly different from that in other European countries [6].

The Civil War moved Spain backwards into a dark age of repression. Her poets were dead or in exile, her greatest musician, Casals, and her greatest painter, Picasso, lived abroad. Spain was the pariah of post-1945 Europe. The vital electric crackle of her life had been stilled and remained stilled for many years. In the 1950s, and with gathering speed in the 1960s and 1970s, Spain's economic progress raised the overall standard of life, but development was still lopsided. In the arts, in the press and in politics, Francoist attitudes persisted; the *Grises*, the grey-clad security forces, still pressed harshly on dissidents, still moved over the Basque Provinces as if they were in occupied territory. By the 1980s, however, most of this had disappeared and even the security forces were given a face-lift, with a new uniform and a new colour. Franco and Francoists had predicted that democracy would bring in its train all the political ills of the Republic and that disaster would come again. That prediction of doom was never fulfilled. A free society has not inevitably brought social and political catastrophe. The Catalans have achieved autonomy, and, more slowly and with more bitterness, so have the Basques. On the Left, the political ogre of the right, the PCE abandoned Stalinism and sought power through the normal constitutional channels. The PSOE rose again, jettisoned Marxism, embraced the market and became a major force in Spanish politics. On the Right, the politics of conspiracy have been replaced by parliamentary groupings and regroupings within the Cortes, although the attempted military coup of February 1981 confirmed that within the Army there were still unreconciled Francoists nostalgically yearning for a return to the good old days. Its failure, and the generally hostile reaction of most Spaniards to the attempt, together with Spain's good fortune in having a monarchy committed to democracy, are clear signs of an unspoken social compact based upon a common determination that 1936 must never come again – a legacy of the Civil War both beneficent and reassuring.

PART FOUR: DOCUMENTS

DOCUMENT 1 THE ASTURIAN INSURRECTION

Accounts of the savagery of the Foreign Legion and the Moors in the Asturias had leaked out and alarmed liberal and left-wing opinion in Spain and in Europe. This account comes from evidence collected by Felix Gordón Ordás, an ex-Minister and supporter of Lerroux, in a report submitted to Prime Minister Lerroux.

THE FORAYS OF VILLAFRIA. The Regulares entered Villafria on October 13th by the Tenderin road. As soon as the news of their arrival came through whole families left their homes and made for the fields. There remained in Villafria only those who could not go, or who were too frightened to move out, some remaining in their own houses, others going to neighbouring houses to be together. It may be that the Regulares were fired on in Villafria by some revolutionaries in flight. Witnesses, who deserve my complete confidence, assure me that absolutely no one fired on the troops from the houses, and, even had they wished to do so, it would have been impossible, as there were practically no arms in the district. This was shown by a fruitless search carried out by the authorities.

The Regulares invaded Villafria with unheard-of violence – I have even been told that they entered with knives – and from the first moment they began to assault houses and to kill and sack all before them. Sr Marco Miranda enumerates a long list of deaths carried out in the houses of Tenderina Baja, Villafria, and San Esteban de las Cruces by the Regulares. The information that I have received coincides in nearly every respect with his horrible facts, and for this reason I have little to say about them. I shall limit myself to giving in detail what occurred in house No. 2 of Villafria, not because my information differs so much from that of Sr Marco Miranda in this case, but because I heard the story from the chauffeur, José Rodríguez González, native of Oviedo and resident of Madrid, who happened to be there casually, for a few days near his mother, and who saved himself from death in that house by throwing himself out of the window.

The mother of this chauffeur, named Severina González, aged seventy-four, lived in house No. 1 of Villafria with a son aged twenty-eight, Celso Rodríguez; a daughter aged twenty-six, Josefa Rodríguez González; the latter's husband, called Germán, aged thirty-two; one grandchild, son of the couple Josefa – Germán, aged fifteen months; and another son-in-law, Joaquin Tulla López, aged fifty, who belonged to Madrid, and there had left his wife and three children while he was looking for work in Asturias. All this family, on hearing that the Regulares were coming, went over to house No. 2. When the chauffeur, José Rodríguez González, who had been spending some days with his parents-in-law in San Esteban de las Cruces, about two kilometres from Villafria, arrived hurriedly in search of his mother, having heard that the Regulares were very near, he found house No. 1 already empty, and barely had time to take shelter in house No. 2. Although ordinarily in this house there lived twenty-five persons, at the moment of the Regulares' entry in Villafria there were only eighteen: the six already named belonging to house No. 1, plus José Rodríguez González; nine members constituting the family of Domingo Franco, a tramwayman, aged fifty; his wife, Carmen Corral, also about the same age; and their seven children, Manuel, Luis, Emiliano, Laina, Laura, Chela, and Benjamina; Casimiro Alvarez, aged seventy-six, owner of the house; and his son-in-law, named Vicente.

A group of about eighteen to twenty Regulares broke down the door of the house and entered it. Nobody had resisted them, much less been aggressive to them. Only some mattresses had been put behind the door, because since the early morning there had been noise of shooting. It was 11 a.m. when the Regulares set foot in the house. Hardly was the door opened than they began to shoot madly at all the people inside. They thus killed Josefa, Celso, Germán, Joaquin, Domingo, Carmen, Manuel, Luis, Emiliano, Laina, Laura, Casimiro, and Vicente. Out of eighteen people, thirteen were dead. José saved himself by throwing himself from a window, Severina, with her grandchild in her arms, by hiding in a corner of the staircase, and Chela and Benjamina, aged seventeen and fourteen respectively, by some means which I have not heard. *I repeat that not one of these persons, neither of the dead nor of the survivors, had fired a single shot nor made the slightest hostile gesture.* The poor old woman, Severina González, who, horrified, saw nearly all her family killed, still remembers with terror, amid the terrible grief of this tragic scene like a witches' Sabbath, the horrifying face of a Moor without more nose than the two nasal orifices. She also remembers that when she came out of her hiding-place there were no more Moroccan soldiers, only a Spanish military man, who appeared to be the chief, and who, when he saw her come out crying, tried to console her, saying that he had arrived late and that now there was no remedy.

Leah Manning, [34], pp. 189–91.

DOCUMENT 2   THE MILITARY RISING OF 18 JULY 1936

Confusion of aims marks the statements broadcast by leaders of the Rising,
ranging from General Franco's bland assertion of Spanish nationalism to
José Maria Pemán's reassertion of Spain's sense of holy mission. The
impassioned rhetoric of the Falangist leader, Onésimo Redondo, suggests
what form the Rising might have taken if José Antonio had survived. The
reality is found in Queipo de Llano's threats.

(a) The movement we are proclaiming has nothing in common with
petty politics; it is a nationalist Spanish movement with the sole aim
of saving Spain. It is said that the movement is against the working
class; precisely the opposite is the case. We are in favour of the
humble class and the middle class. ... Fear nothing, Spanish working
people. Our movement is dangerous only for those who live like
princes, for those who use trade union funds without rendering
accounts, for those who do nothing but attack the republic.
Something has to be done rapidly to save the republic.

General Franco (Broadcast over the *guardia civil* radio, Tetuán, 22 July
1936), R. Fraser, [126], p. 128.

(b) We are fighting totally for Spain and for civilization. Nor are we
fighting alone; 20 centuries of Western Christian Civilization lie
behind us. We are fighting for God, for our land and our dead. ...
It has always been Spain's providential and historic mission to
save the civilized world from all dangers: expelling moors, stopping
turks, baptizing indians. ... Now new turks, red and cruel asiatics,
are again threatening Europe. But Spain, today as yesterday, opposes
them, saves and redeems civilization. Because this is a holy war, a
crusade of civilization. ...

José Maria Pemán, monarchist poet (Broadcast over Seville radio, 15 August
1936), R. Fraser, [126], p. 154.

(c) We know exactly what the fatherland must recover in these moments
– nothing less than itself. ... We were no more than the humiliated
depository, the dregs of crass, failed ideologies, a colony of Russia,
that's to say, a colony of organized barbarity. ...
The Falange's profound preoccupation is to redeem the proletariat.
... Spain is virtually divided; one half made up of the vast army of
those who earn their daily bread by manual labour, who do not love
Spain, who receive no pleasure from belonging to this illustrious
nation. ... We must assure the workers of the spiritual patrimony
which they have lost, winning for them, above all, the satisfaction
and certainty of their daily bread.
Spain must be proletarianized. It must become a people of

workers. ... The capitalists, the rich will be traitors to the fatherland, unworthy members of the state if ... they continue as they have done up to now with their incorrigible egoism, their refusal to look about them at the trail of hunger, scarcity and pain they leave in their wake.

Bread for all, justice for all – these are our slogans and will shortly be put into practice. *¡España, Una! ¡España, Grande! ¡España, Libre! ¡Arriba España!*

Onésimo Redondo, Falange leader (Broadcast over Valladolid radio, 19 July 1936), R. Fraser, [126], p. 115.

(d) In various villages of which I have heard, right-wing people are being held prisoner and threatened with barbarous fates. I want to make known my system with regard to this. For every person killed I shall kill ten and perhaps even exceed this proportion.

The leaders of these village movements may believe that they can flee; they are wrong. Even if they hide beneath the earth, I shall dig them out; even if they're already dead, I shall kill them again.

General Queipo de Llano (Broadcast over Seville radio, 25 July 1936), R. Fraser, [126], p. 128.

(e) I order and command that anyone caught inciting others to strike, or striking himself, shall be shot immediately.

Don't be frightened.

If someone tries to compel you, I authorize you to kill him like a dog and you will be free of all responsibility ...

General Queipo de Llano (Broadcast over Seville radio, 22 July 1936), R. Fraser, [126], p. 128.

DOCUMENT 3   **SPANISH ANARCHISM**

Anarchism was deeply rooted in the soil of Spain, in Aragon, in the Levante and in the villages of Andalusia. It nurtured a vision of a land where the exploitation of class by class would vanish (a), and selfish individualism give way to male bonding (b). A blueprint of this new society was drawn up by Isaac Puente, its most outstanding contemporary theoretician, in his The Political and Economic Organisation of Society *(c). How this worked out in practice, in post-Rising Spain, may be seen in a charter for a typical rural collective (d).*

(a) Two Anarchist Poems

> Politics is poison
> To him who works the land.
> It is the sponger's tool.
> There is nothing good
> In eating the fruit of someone else's labour.
> To defend capital
> With complete malice
> Thwarts justice
> And perpetuates evil.
>
> Where do you go, bags and all,
> In such haste that I see you running?
> To the congress of the anarchists
> To speak and make myself understood.
> What does the anarchist wish to say?
> The great phalanx of workers
> Reclaims its right to live:
> Under the red flag, we must
> overcome
> Exploitation.

Jerome R. Mintz, [110], pp. 139 and 145.

(b) *Testimony of Manuel Llamas, a faísta of Medina Sidonia, Cadiz Province. He was a member of one of the three grupos de afinidad in the town in the 1930s.*

> I was thirteen when I joined the CNT, and when I was eighteen or nineteen I became a member of the FAI. It was all secret, to keep out the uninformed. We would talk to each other to see if we had the same idea. After four or five words one can see if there's an affinity, if one has trust. It's like love between a man and a woman – they meet and after only a few words they know. Each group had ten or fewer members. When the number reached ten, another group was formed. The essence of the FAI was the idea of liberty. We were to propagate anarchism in order to emancipate the worker. We would propagandise among the youth – books, newspapers, talks – sowing education.

Jerome R Mintz, [110], p. 140.

(c) Libertarian communism is based upon the economic organization of society, the economic interests being the only kind of social link upon which the interests of all individuals converge. The social organization has no other goal but to *place in common possession* whatever constitutes social wealth (the means of production and the distribution of goods and services) and to make the obligation to contribute to production a common obligation from everyone according to his ability. All *non-economic* affairs and functions will be left to the private initiative and activity of the individuals and their voluntary groupings without outside interference.

Libertarian communism is the organization of society without the State and without capitalist property relations. To establish libertarian communism it will not be necessary to invent artificial forms of social organization. The new society will emerge 'from the shell of the old'. The elements of the future society are already planted in the existing order. They are the Syndicate and the Free Commune (sometimes called 'Free Municipality') which are old, deeply rooted non-statist popular institutions spontaneously organized, and embracing all towns and villages in both urban and rural areas. The Free Commune is also ideally suited to cope successfully with the problems of social and economic life in libertarian rural communities. Within the Free Commune there is also room for cooperative associations of artisans, farmers and other groups or individuals who prefer to remain independent or form their own associations to meet their own needs (providing of course that they do not exploit hired labor for wages).

Both the Syndicates and the Free Communes, in accordance with federative and democratic procedures, will, by mutual agreement, be free to conduct their own affairs within their own spheres, without interference from any outside authority. This will not be necessary because the workers will, from sheer necessity, (if for no other reason) be obliged to establish their own Federations of Industries to coordinate their multiform economic activities.

Through their syndicates, their Free Communes and their subsidiary coordinating agencies, the workers will take collective possession of all private (not personal) property and collectively administer production and consumption of goods and public services locally, regionally and nationally.

The terms 'Libertarian' and 'Communism' denote the fusion of two inseparable concepts, the indispensable prerequisites for the free society: collectivism and individual freedom.

Sam Dolgoff, [101], pp. 28–31.

(d)   STATUTES OF THE WORKERS' FREE COLLECTIVE OF
TAMARITE DE LITERA

Article 1. With the title of Collective and cooperative, there has been set up in Tamarite on October 1, 1936 a Collective composed of peasants and industrial workers with the aim of exploiting collectively the agricultural properties and industrial enterprises formerly belonging to factious elements who participated directly or indirectly in the fascist uprising in Spain and whose goods thus pass to the Collective. Also included in this action of collective exploitation are the goods of collectivists and of property owners or industrial enterprises which have remained loyal and in agreement with the revolutionary movement, as well as the goods of those who, without being fascists, do not properly farm their land or do not use their own labour, or have stopped cultivating their land.

Art. 2. Our Collective composed of, as we have already said, peasants and industrial workers, will be guided by humane sentiments and the noblest social principles.

Art. 3. The ends aimed at by the constitution of this Collective shall be: the improvement of the social and economic condition of the mass of peasants and industrial workers who have always struggled for the ideas of social recognition both before the fascist uprising and during the revolution.

ASSETS OF THE COLLECTIVE
Art. 4. The assets of the Collective shall consist of all properties, urban, rural as well as of the goods expropriated from fascist elements, and the goods of the Collective itself and of those who, without being fascist, do not properly cultivate their land by their own efforts.

Art. 5. In no case will the assets of the Collective be broken up, whether they come from fascists or from voluntary members. Land will be cultivated in common by a single community which will divide into three or more sections; each section or delineated zone will dispose of all the equipment needed for agricultural work, working animals, tools; each group will nominate its technical delegates to ensure the best use of the expropriated estates.

(a) As already stated, the workers will be divided into three sections, or more, according to individual aptitudes; some to attend to the olive trees and the various fruit trees, others for harvesting lucerne and cereals, others for land work with spade or hoe, others to handle the mules, others on minor tasks; by this organisation we shall eliminate weak points and shortcomings of which we are only too well aware.

(b) Every collectivist is authorised to belong to whichever section he wishes and will then be able to change domicile with his family; all will have the obligation to carry out the instructions of the responsible delegates who will have decided at preliminary meetings on the work to be done; if anyone does not apply the agreements made in those meetings the administrative Commission will be informed by the responsible delegate who will decide on the expulsion of the comrade or comrades who have adopted that position.

(c) The groups previously constituted will have the right to carry on, according to the already established constitution.

(d) All those who won 3½ hectares of irrigated land as well as of dry land will be free to join the Collective or to be individualists, but they will be allowed to cultivate their land only by their own efforts; however both collectivists and individualists will have to help in the ways asked of them by the community, by bringing their working animals as well as their personal effort. Those possessing less than 3½ hectares will have to join the Collective.

(e) Each group as well as each collectivist will receive from the management commission a book in which will be entered income and outgoings.

RIGHTS AND DUTIES OF THE COLLECTIVE

Art. 12. The Collective puts at the service of collectivists the general consumers' cooperative which deals with all needs: food, drinks, heating, clothing; equally it assures medical and pharmaceutical services and everything concerning collective needs and development; it also disposes of four oil crushers, one flour mill, a soap factory (in conjunction with oil crushers for the production of lower grade oil), a lye factory, three lime kilns, three for ceramics and bricks, and one electricity generator.

Art. 13. Every collectivist has the right to rear pigs, hens, turkeys, geese, rabbits, where he lives, in order to assure a surplus. 10% of the poultry and rabbits will be handed over to the collectivist units, and any surplus eggs will be passed to the cooperative in order to supply those workers engaged in industrial work and all those who may need them until such time as the new collective units can produce them for themselves.

Art. 14. All collectivists working in industry and all those who, not being agricultural workers, cannot cultivate vegetables will receive supplies for themselves and their families free of charge.

Art. 15. The Collective guarantees to the head of each family a weekly wage in local money. The scale of payments in local money is as follows:

A young couple	25.00 pesetas
An old couple	21.00 pesetas
Three adults	33.00 pesetas
For each additional person	1.00 peseta per day
For each minor	0.70 peseta per day
For two single women	20.00 pesetas per week
For a single man	18.00 pesetas per week
For a single woman	14.00 pesetas per week
For those taking their meals at the Collective's canteen	9.00 pesetas

Art. 16. All members of the Collective, without sex discrimination, will have to work from the age of fourteen to sixty except in cases of physical disability medically confirmed; in such cases work will be voluntary and not obligatory.

Art. 17. Expenses for medical treatment, medicaments, light and shelter are borne by the Collective, as well as supplies of edible oil for the whole year.

Art. 18. When a member of the Collective takes a companion, that is to say, wishes to start a new family, the Collective guarantees her material needs.

Art. 20. Every collectivist comrade will have the inalienable right of withdrawing from the Collective whenever he wishes to do so; but 15% of the value of the assets that he brought on joining will be retained.

Gaston Leval, [107], pp. 215–18.

DOCUMENT 4   **FALANGISM**

On the Right, the traditional parties offered no model for social change. The only exception was the Falange where the ideas of José Antonio, Ledesma and Redondo merged to produce a programme marked by social concern and by a genuine compassion. In the twenty-six points of the Falange proclaimed in November 1934 a fusty imperialism mingled with (to the Right) an alarmingly progressive social programme, as shown particularly in points X, XII, XV, XIX.

(a)   GUIDELINES OF THE FALANGE:
                        THE 26 POINTS

                    NATION. DESTINY. EMPIRE

I. We believe in the supreme reality of Spain. Its strengthening, elevation and aggrandizement is the urgent collective task of all Spaniards. The accomplishment of this task must have relentless priority over all individual, group or class interests.

II. Spain is an indivisible destiny in universal terms. Any plot against this indivisible whole is repulsive. All separatism is a crime we shall not forgive.

The prevailing constitution, in so far as it foments disintegration, offends against the indivisible nature of Spain's destiny. We therefore insist that it be repealed forthwith.

III. We are committed to the empire. We declare that Spain's historical fulfilment is the empire. We demand for Spain a prominent position in Europe. We will not tolerate either international isolation nor foreign interference.

Regarding the countries of Spanish America, our aim is the unification of culture, economic interests and power. Spain lays claim to being the spiritual axis of the Spanish-speaking world on the grounds of her predominance in world affairs.

IV. Our armed forces – on land, at sea and in the air – must be sufficiently strong and efficient to secure total independence and a fitting world status for Spain at all times. We shall give back to the land, sea and air forces all the public dignity they merit and we shall see to it that a martial outlook pervades all Spanish life in their image. ...

VI. Ours will be a totalitarian state in the service of the fatherland's integrity. All Spaniards will play a part therein through their membership of families, municipalities and trade unions. None shall play a part therein through a political party. The system of political parties will be resolutely abolished, together with all its corollaries: inorganic suffrage, representation by conflicting factions and the Cortes as we know it. ...

THE ECONOMY. WORK. THE CLASS STRUGGLE

IX. In the economic sphere, we think of Spain as one huge syndicate of all those engaged in production. We shall organise Spanish society along corporative lines, by means of a system of vertical unions representing the various branches of production, in the service of national economic integrity.

X. We reject the capitalist system, which disregards the needs of the people, dehumanizes private property and transforms the workers into shapeless masses prone to misery and despair. Our spiritual and national awareness likewise rejects Marxism. We shall channel the drive of the working classes, nowadays led astray by Marxism, and demand their direct participation in the formidable task of the national state. ...

XII. The primary purpose of wealth is to effect an improvement in the standard of living of all the people – and this will be the declared policy of our state. It is intolerable that great masses of people live in poverty, while a few enjoy every luxury. ...

XV. All Spanish citizens are entitled to employment. The public institutions will provide for the maintenance of those who are involuntarily out of work.

XVI. Every Spaniard who is not an invalid is duty bound to work. The National Syndicalist state will not have the slightest regard for those who do not fulfil any function, but expect to live like guests at the expense of other people's efforts.

XVII. We must at all costs raise the standard of living in the rural areas, on which Spain will always depend for her food. For this reason we commit ourselves to the strict implementation of an economic and social reform of agriculture.

XVIII. We shall strengthen agricultural production (economic reform) by means of the following measures:

By guaranteeing the farmer an adequate minimum price for all his produce.

By seeing to it that much of what is nowadays absorbed by the cities in payment for their intellectual and commercial services is returned to the land, in order to endow rural areas sufficiently.

By organising a real system of national agricultural credit which will lend the farmers money at low rates of interest, thereby freeing them from usury and patronage.

By spreading education pertaining to matters of agriculture and animal husbandry.

By rationalizing production according to the suitability of the land and the outlets available for the various products.

By promoting a protectionist tariff policy covering agriculture and the raising of cattle.

By speeding up the construction of a hydraulic network.

By rationalizing the size of holdings, with the elimination both of vast estates that are not fully exploited and smallholdings that are uneconomic by reason of their low output.

XIX. We shall achieve a social organization of agriculture by means of the following measures:

By redistributing all the arable land so as to promote family holdings and by giving farmers every encouragement to join the union.

By rescuing the masses of people, who are exhausting themselves scratching on barren soil, from their present poverty and transferring them to new holdings of arable land. ...

EDUCATION. RELIGION

XXIII. It is a fundamental mission of the state to impose a rigorous discipline on education which will produce a stout national spirit and fill the souls of future generations with joyful pride in their fatherland.

All men will receive pre-military training to prepare them for the honour of admission to Spain's national and popular armed forces.

XXIV. Culture will be organized in such a way that no talent will go to waste for lack of finance. All the deserving will have easy access even to higher education.

XXV. Our movement integrates the Catholic religion – traditionally glorious and predominant in Spain – into national reconstruction.

The Church and the state will agree by concordat on the delimitation of their respective spheres, but that does not mean that any interference from the Church will be tolerated nor any activity likely to undermine the dignity of the state or the integrity of the nation.

THE NATIONAL REVOLUTION

XXVI. The Spanish Falange of the J.O.N.S. wants the establishment of a new order, as set out in the foregoing principles. So that it may prevail in the conflict with the present order, the Spanish Falange aims at a national revolution.

Its style will be trenchant, ardent and militant. Life is a militia and must be lived in a spirit purified by service and sacrifice.

Hugh Thomas, [22], pp. 132–7.

(b) *A voice from within*
  Dionisio Ridruejo was a Falangist who, like José Antonio, thought that Falangism offered a radical solution to Spain's social problems, a middle way between liberalism and marxism. He rose to become propaganda chief under Franco, and then became increasingly disenchanted with the lack of any genuine social reform.

I was coming to realise that the revolution we had hoped to make was impossible. Eighty per cent of those being executed in the reararguard were workers. The repression was aimed at decimating the working class, destroying its power. In eliminating those whom our revolution was to benefit, the purpose of the revolution itself was eliminated. The reasoning behind the necessity for the purge was the sophism (shared moreover by both sides) that the enemy was a minority which was forcing the great mass of those on the other side to fight. Destroy that minority and order would be restored. The repression on the nationalist side was carried out in cold blood, purposefully and methodically, to destroy that 'minority'. It was a class war. Not everyone, certainly not the petty bourgeoisie on the nationalist side, recognised it as such, or they would have been on the other side. But the ruling class certainly knew it. Franco was its most lucid exponent, his crusade was another way of expressing it. ...

R. Fraser, [126], p. 320.

DOCUMENT 5   **TERROR ON THE LEFT**

There are many well-documented accounts of the paseo *which disgraced the Republican zones in the earliest part of the war. This account is by an American journalist, H. Edward Knoblaugh, who was in Madrid during the summer of 1936.*

Many mornings, after breakfast, Pedro Rosales, the Anarchist chauffeur the government had assigned to us with the requisitioned car we had at our service, and I, used to make the rounds of the outskirts of Madrid to check up on the *paseo* victims of the night before.

Singly and in clusters they lay alongside the roadway, riddled with bullets. The wooded Casa de Campo, former playground of the king, was a favourite execution spot before it came under Rebel fire. University City, called the finest university campus in Europe, never failed to produce at least ten or twelve *fiambres* – Spanish for cold meats – each day. Some of the bodies were horribly mutilated. Some were left with pieces of cardboard on their chests on which were scrawled the alleged offences for which they had been killed. In the first days of anti-clerical outrages there were many bodies of priests and nuns among the victims. We generally could identify them by the scapulars, rosaries or bits of religious clothing jammed into their mouths by their executioners. Some of the victims were lined up against a wall in firing-squad style. Others were told to run and were shot down like rabbits as they zigzagged away. Women, leading children by the hand, sometimes went out to see the *fiambres*. And I have seen the children vomit on looking at the gruesome sights. Pedro, the chauffeur, was one of the hardest-looking individuals it has ever been my lot to know, but he had a weaker stomach than any of the children. He positively refused to come anywhere near the bodies. Pedro said his Andalusian origin made him leery about seeing dead people. The Andalusians are probably the most superstitious race in the world.

During the first weeks the death-carts did not come around to collect these bodies until nearly noon. Later they started at dawn and had them all removed by 8 o'clock in the morning. Sometimes they would miss one or two. By the time they got around next day decomposition had a good start. Workmen finding bodies some distance from the city would bury them on the spot or at least give them a shallow covering of earth as they lay on the ground.

As the death-carts lumbered toward the morgue, the feet of the stacked dead sticking out the rear like timber-butts, men and women would fall in line behind them and follow them into the death house to see if a friend or relative were among the victims. There they were allowed to look over the gruesome assembly at their leisure. Sometimes the faces had been shot away and identification would have to be made by fishing through the pockets of the putrid cadavers. This task was left strictly to the anxious ones, and many fainted and had to be taken out of the foul place. I went only once, with another newspaperman. I shall not forget the scrawny old morgue-keeper and her toothless grin as she cackled: 'Business is poor, boys, only eighty today.' The dead were buried in trenches, twenty or thirty in a pile, after twenty-four hours in the charnel-house.

H. Edward Knoblaugh, [131], pp. 72–4.

DOCUMENT 6   **TERROR ON THE RIGHT**

On the Nationalist side, terror was more integrated into the policy of the new regime and was undertaken with official approval. This account describes, in the words of the French Catholic writer, Georges Bernanos, what happened when Majorca was 'purged' by the Nationalists. 'Count' Rossi, who organised the repression in Majorca, was in fact Arconaldo Bonaccorsi, the successor to the Marqués de Zayas, head of the local Falangists, under whose command the round-ups described in the first extract took place.

(a) I used to see on the Ramblas in Majorca trucks crowded with men. These trucks roared past with the sound of thunder, on a level with the many-coloured terraces, lavishly equipped and gleaming, gay with the murmurs of a country fair. These trucks were grey with the dust of the road, grey too with the men who sat there four by four, their grey caps upside down on their knees and their hands lying gently along the seams of their trousers. They were rounded up every evening from forgotten villages, at the hour when they came from the fields; and they set off on their last journey, their shirts clinging to their shoulders with sweat, their arms full of the day's toil, leaving the soup on the table and a woman who had arrived too late at the garden gate, with a little bundle of possessions twisted in a new napkin: *A Dios! recuerdos!*

(b) The newcomer was neither a general, nor a count, nor was he called Rossi: he was simply an Italian official belonging to the Blackshirts. One fine morning we saw him arriving in a scarlet three-engined plane. His first visit was to the military governor, nominated by General Goded. He was received politely by the governor and his officers. Hammering the table with his fist, he made a speech declaring that he was the herald of the spirit of Fascism, and a few days later the general together with his entire staff was thrown into the prison of San Carlos, while Count Rossi assumed effective control of the Falange. Wearing a black shirt with an enormous white cross blazoned on the breast, he drove through the villages, taking the wheel of his racing car, while other cars filled with men armed to the teeth followed in clouds of dust. Every morning the newspapers provided complete descriptions of these oratorical journeys, where in an extraordinary mixture of the languages of Majorca, Italy and Spain, the Count, flanked by the local mayor and curate, announced his Crusade. No doubt the Italian government possessed some less garish collaborators in Palma than this huge ruffian who, while wiping his hands on the tablecloth during a dinner with a great lady of Palma society, declared that he had to have at least 'one woman a day'. But the particular mission entrusted with him agreed well with his genius. His mission was the organisation of terror.

From then on every night teams recruited by him operated in the villages and in the suburbs of Palma. Wherever these men demonstrated their zeal, the scene was nearly always the same. There was the same discreet knock on the door of a comfortable apartment or of a thatched cottage, the same trampling of feet in a garden filled with shadows or funereal whispering on the landing, with some poor devil listening through the wall, ear pressed against a keyhole, heart shaking with terror – 'Follow us!' The same words to the woman driven out of her mind, her hands trembling as she gathers together those small familiar possessions put down a few moments before, and the noise of the motor still filling the air with its thunder out there, in the street. 'I shouldn't wake the children, should I? It wouldn't be any use. You are taking me to prison, señor?' '*Perfectamente*,' says the killer, who is sometimes only twenty years old. And then they climb into the truck, where two or three comrades have already taken their places, equally resigned, equally melancholy, with a vagueness in their eyes. ... *Hombre!* The truck makes a grinding noise and starts off. As long as it keeps to the main road, there is still a gleam of hope. But already they are slowing down, over the rough, bumpy hollow of a small earth road. 'Get out!' So they jump out, line up, kiss a medal or only a thumbnail. Bang! Bang! Bang! The bodies are arranged along the slope where the gravedigger will find them the next day, head shattered and the nape of the neck lying on a hideous cushion of black coagulated blood. I speak of the gravedigger because they are very careful to do what has to be done close to a cemetery. The local mayor will inscribe in his records: 'So-and-so, died of cerebral congestion ...'.

The first phase of the process of liquidation lasted for four months. During the course of these four months the stranger who was chiefly responsible for these killings sat in the place of honour during all the religious celebrations. He was usually accompanied by a chaplain recruited locally, wearing boots and breeches, with a white cross on his chest, pistols in his belt. (This priest, as it happened, was later shot by the military.) No one was permitted to remain in doubt about the discretionary powers of the Italian general. I know a poor priest who humbly begged him to spare the lives of three young women prisoners who had come from Mexico. He had heard their confessions and believed them to be good people. 'Very well,' said the Count, who was about to go to bed, 'I will discuss the matter with my pillow.' The following day he ordered his men to kill the women.

So it was that right up to December the sunken roads of the island in the neighbourhood of the cemeteries, regularly received their mournful harvest of people whose thoughts found no merit in the eyes of the authorities. They were workers and peasants, but they were also middle-class people, druggists, lawyers. When I asked a doctor friend for the film taken some time before by a radiologist who was one of his colleagues – he was the only radiologist in Palma – he replied smiling: 'I wonder whether we shall ever find it. ... Poor X was taken on a little journey a few days ago. ...' These facts are known to everyone.

Robert Payne, [75], pp. 106–7.

DOCUMENT 7   **THE MILITIAS**

Lack of training and equipment were the two outstanding characteristics of the militias and explain their early failures and their great losses. Orwell describes here the POUM militia's preparations for battle.

I have spoken of the militia 'uniform', which probably gives a wrong impression. It was not exactly a uniform. Perhaps a 'multiform' would be the proper name for it. Everyone's clothes followed the same general plan, but they were never quite the same in any two cases. Practically everyone in the army wore corduroy knee-breeches, but there the uniformity ended. Some wore puttees, others corduroy gaiters, others leather leggings or high boots. Everyone wore a zipper jacket, but some of the jackets were of leather, others of wool and of every conceivable colour. The kinds of cap were about as numerous as their wearers. It was usual to adorn the front of your cap with a party badge, and in addition nearly every man wore a red or red and black handkerchief round his throat. A militia column at that time was an extraordinary-looking rabble. But the clothes had to be issued as this or that factory rushed them out, and they were not bad clothes considering the circumstances. The shirts and socks were wretched cotton things, however, quite useless against cold. I hate to think of what the militiamen must have gone through in the earlier months before anything was organized. I remember coming upon a newspaper of only about two months earlier in which one of the P.O.U.M. leaders, after a visit to the front, said that he would try to see to it that 'every militiaman had a blanket'. A phrase to make you shudder if you have ever slept in a trench.

On my second day at the barracks there began what was comically called 'instruction'. At the beginning there were frightful scenes of chaos. The recruits were mostly boys of sixteen or seventeen from the back streets of Barcelona, full of revolutionary ardour but completely ignorant of the meaning of war. It was impossible even to get them to stand in line. Discipline did not exist; if a man disliked an order he would step out of the ranks and argue fiercely with the officer. The lieutenant who instructed us was a stout, fresh-faced, pleasant young man who had previously been a Regular Army officer, and still looked like one, with his smart carriage and spick-and-span uniform. Curiously enough he was a sincere and ardent Socialist. Even more than the men themselves he insisted upon complete social equality between all ranks. I remember his pained surprise when an ignorant recruit addressed him as 'Señor'. 'What! Señor? Who is that calling me Señor? Are we not all comrades?' I doubt whether it made his job any easier. Meanwhile the raw recruits were getting no military training that could be of the slightest use to them. I had been told that foreigners were not obliged to attend 'instruction' (the Spaniards, I noticed, had a pathetic belief that all foreigners knew more of military matters than themselves), but naturally I turned out with the others. I was very anxious to learn how to use a machine-gun; it was a weapon I had never had a chance to handle. To my dismay I found that we were taught nothing about the use of weapons. The so-called instruction was simply parade-ground drill of the most antiquated, stupid kind; right turn, left turn, about turn, marching at attention in column of threes and all the rest of that useless nonsense which I had learned when I was fifteen years old. It was an extraordinary form for the training of a guerilla army to take. Obviously if you have only a few days in which to train a soldier, you must teach him the things he will most need; how to take cover, how to advance across open ground, how to mount guards and build a parapet – above all, how to use his weapons. Yet this mob of eager children, who were going to be thrown into the front line in a few days' time, were not even taught how to fire a rifle or pull the pin out of a bomb. At the time I did not grasp that this was because there were no weapons to be had. In the P.O.U.M. militia the shortage of rifles was so desperate that fresh troops reaching the front always had to take their rifles from the troops they relieved in the line. In the whole of the Lenin Barracks there were, I believe, no rifles except those used by the sentries.

George Orwell, [135], p. 12.

DOCUMENT 8   **THE INTERNATIONAL BRIGADES**

Jason Gurney's account of the battle of Jarama paints a picture of a Brigade staff with no maps and dependent upon reports in four different languages. The higher command was often incompetent and the Internationals, the

XVth, suffered heavy losses. This passage suggests the scepticism with which pronouncements from the top came to be viewed.

The Company and Platoon Commanders rejoined their units and explained the situation to their men. During the afternoon I went up to the front trench line to arrange my observation post and telephone line. I found everyone roaring with laughter.

'Have you heard the news, Comrade? We are about to make a glorious attack.'

'Yes, indeed, Comrade. The aviation will destroy the enemy's line at sunrise.'

'It'll be the first time that we've seen any planes on this front.'

'Ah, but, Comrade, this time it is going to be different.'

'Yes, Comrade, this time it is going to be entirely different.'

'And the massed artillery will lay down a barrage of tremendous power.'

'I haven't seen any artillery.'

'But you will, Comrade. This will be supported by a considerable force of tanks.'

'Well, by Jesus, I hope you're right.'

'We must have faith in our glorious revolutionary leadership.'

'Copic?'

'Yes, Comrade. Our glorious leader, the Comrade Brigade Commander Copic, has given his personal assurance. Our advance will be irresistible.'

Jason Gurney, [128], p. 154.

DOCUMENT 9   **A BRITISH VOLUNTEER WITH THE NATIONALISTS**

Peter Kemp, a Cambridge graduate, joined the Carlists, and was one of the very few volunteers to fight on Franco's side. He was transferred to the Foreign Legion and when this incident took place was serving under Colonel Peñaredonda, notorious for his evil temper and his hatred of the International Brigades.

The following day remains in my memory for one of the most horrible incidents in my experience.

The horror of it is still with me as I write; nor, I fear, will it ever leave me. I can scarcely bear to write of it now. At noon next day we were still resting on our cliff-top when I was ordered to report to Cancela. I found him talking with some legionaries who had brought in a deserter from the International Brigades – an Irishman from Belfast; he had given himself up to one of our patrols down by the river. Cancela wanted me to interrogate him. The man explained that he had been a seaman on a British ship trading to Valencia, where he had got very drunk one night, missed his ship and been picked up by the police. The next thing he knew, he was in Albacete, impressed into the International Brigades. He knew that if he tried to escape in Republican Spain he would certainly be retaken and shot; and so he had bided his time until he reached the front, when he had taken the first opportunity to desert. He had been wandering around for two days before he found our patrol.

I was not absolutely sure that he was telling the truth; but I knew that if I seemed to doubt his story he would be shot, and I was resolved to do everything in my power to save his life. Translating his account to Cancela, I urged that this was indeed a special case; the man was a deserter, not a prisoner, and we should be unwise as well as unjust to shoot him. Moved either by my arguments, or by consideration for my feelings, Cancela agreed to spare him, subject to de Mora's consent; I had better go and see de Mora at once while Cancela would see that the deserter had something to eat. De Mora was sympathetic. 'You seem to have a good case,' he said. 'Unfortunately my orders from Colonel Peñaredonda are to shoot all foreigners. If you can get his consent I'll be delighted to let the man off. You'll find the Colonel over there, on the highest of those hills. Take the prisoner with you, in case there are any questions, and your two runners as escort.'

It was an exhausting walk of nearly a mile with the midday sun blazing on our backs.

'Does it get any hotter in this country?' the deserter asked as we panted up the steep sides of a ravine, the sweat pouring down our faces and backs.

'You haven't seen the half of it yet. Wait another three months,' I answered, wondering grimly whether I should be able to win him even another three hours of life.

I found Colonel Peñaredonda sitting cross-legged with a plate of fried eggs on his knee. He greeted me amiably enough as I stepped forward and saluted; I had taken care to leave the prisoner well out of earshot. I repeated his story, adding my own plea at the end, as I had with Cancela and de Mora. 'I have the fellow here, sir,' I concluded, 'in case you wish to ask him any questions.' The Colonel did not look up from his plate: 'No, Peter,' he said casually, his mouth full of egg, 'I don't want to ask him anything. Just take him away and shoot him.'

I was so astonished that my mouth dropped open; my heart seemed to stop beating. Peñaredonda looked up, his eyes full of hatred:

'Get out!' he snarled. 'You heard what I said.' As I withdrew he shouted after me: 'I warn you, I intend to see that this order is carried out.'

Motioning the prisoner and escort to follow, I started down the hill; I would not walk with them, for I knew that he would question me and I could not bring myself to speak. I decided not to tell him until the last possible moment, so that at least he might be spared the agony of waiting. I even thought of telling him to try to make a break for it while I distracted the escorts' attention; then I remembered Peñaredonda's parting words and, looking back, saw a pair of legionaries following us at a distance. I was so numb with misery and anger that I didn't notice where I was going until I found myself in front of de Mora once more. When I told him the news he bit his lip:

'Then I'm afraid there's nothing we can do,' he said gently. 'You had better carry out the execution yourself. Someone has got to do it, and it will be easier for him to have a fellow-countryman around. After all, he knows that you have tried to save him. Try to get it over quickly.'

It was almost more than I could bear to face the prisoner, where he stood between my two runners. As I approached they dropped back a few paces, leaving us alone; they were good men and understood what I was feeling. I forced myself to look at him. I am sure he knew what I was going to say.

'I've got to shoot you.' A barely audible 'Oh my God!' escaped him.

Briefly I told him how I had tried to save him. I asked him if he wanted a priest, or a few minutes by himself, and if there were any messages he wanted me to deliver.

'Nothing,' he whispered, 'please make it quick.'

'That I can promise you. Turn round and start walking straight ahead.'

He held out his hand and looked me in the eyes, saying only: 'Thank you.'

'God bless you!' I murmured.

As he turned his back and walked away I said to my two runners: 'I beg you to aim true. He must not feel anything.' They nodded, and raised their rifles. I looked away. The two shots exploded simultaneously.

'On our honour, sir,' the senior of the two said to me, 'he could not have felt a thing.'

Peter Kemp, [130], pp. 170–2.

DOCUMENT 10   **DEFENCE OF MADRID**

Henry Buckley, an English reporter, pays tribute to the citizens of the capital, the Madrileños.

Yet down by Toledo Bridge talking to old Colonel Mena, who must have been well over sixty and who had fought gallantly all the way back from Toledo, I saw a sight which made me very ashamed of my petty worries about myself. Going up into line were long files of civilians. They had no uniforms. Just ordinary suits and a rifle slung anyhow over the shoulder. Most of the rifles were aged and I should say were nearly as unsafe for the man who fired as for the enemy. Some of the rifles had not even a bandolier and their owners had improvised one with string. Each man was given a handful of cartridges which he had to carry as best he could. Most of them had pockets in which to stow them but a few who wore overalls had to carry them in their hands.

They were just men called up by the trade unions and the political organisations to fight for Madrid. Many of them did not even know how to handle a rifle. On my way back into town I passed a news reel theatre which normally was open all day. I asked if the show was to be as usual. The girl at the cash desk was not sure. One of the operators had gone to fight but the other one was awaiting orders. It seemed that there were only a limited number of rifles. If the second man was told to stay at his post then, of course, the show would go on. At the Gran Vía Hotel, half the waiters had gone.

Believe me, those were the men who saved Madrid. It was not General Miaja, nor the International Brigades. There were those two critical days of November 7 and 8 when the situation hung in the balance. It was the courage and sacrifice of the Madrid people which alone held the feeble lines which separated Franco from the city. Many of them died, unknown and unsung. Tram-drivers and café waiters are not personages whose names make news. Of those who were known, there was Emilio Barrado, one of Spain's best sculptors. He went down with a group as 'political commissioner' to give what the Americans call 'pep talks' to the men. He told a friend of mine that in the first few days the men could only be given fifty cartridges to last them twenty-four hours. Supplies did not run to more. These men had no sanitary services, no regular food supplies, often they had neither trained officers, nor non-commissioned officers. Yet they held the pick of the Nationalist Army, the highly trained Tercio, the well-disciplined Moorish corps, the fanatical Carlists from Navarre. They just stayed doggedly in the positions in which they were put and fired their rifles blindly at the foe, when they could see him.

Henry Buckley, [122], pp. 262–3.

DOCUMENT 11   REVOLUTIONARY BARCELONA

Orwell's famous account of the city en fête, overcome by revolutionary euphoria.

I mention this Italian militiaman because he has stuck vividly in my memory. With his shabby uniform and fierce pathetic face he typifies for me the special atmosphere of that time. He is bound up with all my memories of that period of the war – the red flags in Barcelona, the gaunt trains full of shabby soldiers creeping to the front, the grey war-stricken towns farther up the line, the muddy, ice-cold trenches in the mountains.

This was in late December 1936, less than seven months ago as I write, and yet it is a period that has already receded into enormous distance. Later events have obliterated it much more completely than they have obliterated 1935, or 1905, for that matter. I had come to Spain with some notion of writing newspaper articles, but I had joined the militia almost immediately, because at that time and in that atmosphere it seemed the only conceivable thing to do. The Anarchists were still in virtual control of Catalonia and the revolution was still in full swing. To anyone who had been there since the beginning it probably seemed even in December or January that the revolutionary period was ending; but when one came straight from England the aspect of Barcelona was something startling and overwhelming. It was the first time that I had ever been in a town where the working class was in the saddle. Practically every building of any size had been seized by the workers and was draped with red flags or with the red and black flag of the Anarchists; every wall was scrawled with the hammer and sickle and with the initials of the revolutionary parties; almost every church had been gutted and its images burnt. Churches here and there were being systematically demolished by gangs of workmen. Every shop and café had an inscription saying that it had been collectivized; even the bootblacks had been collectivized and their boxes painted red and black. Waiters and shop-walkers looked you in the face and treated you as an equal. Servile and even ceremonial forms of speech had temporarily disappeared. Nobody said 'Señor, or 'Don' or even 'Usted'; everyone called everyone else 'Comrade' and 'Thou', and said 'Salud!' instead of 'Buenos días'. Tipping was forbidden by law; almost my first experience was receiving a lecture from a hotel manager for trying to tip a lift-boy. There were no private motor-cars, they had all been commandeered, and all the trams and taxis and much of the other transport were painted red and black. The revolutionary posters were everywhere, flaming from the walls in clean reds and blues that made the few remaining advertisements look like daubs of mud. Down the Ramblas, the wide central artery of the town where crowds of people streamed constantly to and fro, the loudspeakers were bellowing revolutionary songs all day and far into the night. And it was the aspect of crowds that was the queerest thing of all. In outward appearance it was a town in which the wealthy classes had practically ceased to exist. Except for a small number of women and foreigners there were no 'well-dressed' people at all. Practically everyone wore rough working-class clothes, or blue overalls, or some variant of the militia uniform. All this was queer and moving. There was much in it that I did not understand, in some ways I did not even like it, but I recognized it immediately as a state of affairs worth fighting for. Also I believed that things were as they appeared, that this was really a workers' State and that the entire bourgeoisie had either fled, been killed, or voluntarily come over to the workers' side; I did not realize that great numbers of well-to-do bourgeois were simply lying low and disguising themselves as proletarians for the time being.

George Orwell, [135], pp. 8–9.

DOCUMENT 12   THE DESTRUCTION OF GUERNICA

An eye-witness account by Father Alberto de Onaindía of the most famous incident of the war, the German bombing of the small Basque town of Guernica. This was the emotional heartland of the Basque Provinces, with its Tree of Guernica, the oak under which the Basque Parliament traditionally met. Luis Bolín, chief of the foreign press section at Salamanca, claimed immediately that the destruction of the town was the work of retreating militia, a claim he repeated as recently as 1967 when his memoirs Spain, the Vital Years *[118], were published.*

Late in the afternoon of April 26th I was going by car to rescue my mother and my sisters, then living in Marquina, a town about to fall into the hands of Franco. It was one of those magnificently clear days, the sky soft and serene. We reached the outskirts of Guernica just before five o'clock. The streets were busy with the traffic of market day. Suddenly we heard the siren, and trembled. People were running about in all directions, abandoning everything they possessed, some hurrying into the shelters, others running into the hills. Soon an enemy aeroplane appeared over Guernica. A peasant was passing by. 'It's nothing, only one of the "white" ones,' he said. 'He'll drop a few bombs, and then he'll go away.' The Basques had learned to distinguish between the twin-engined 'whites' and the three-engined 'blacks'. The 'white' aeroplane made a reconnaissance over the town, and when he was directly over the centre he dropped three bombs. Immediately afterwards he saw a squadron of seven planes followed a little later by six more, and this in turn by a third squadron of five more. All of them were Junkers. Meanwhile Guernica was seized with a terrible panic.

I left the car by the side of the road and took refuge with five *milicianos* in a sewer. The water came up to our ankles. From our hiding-place we could see everything that happened without being seen. The aeroplanes came low, flying at two hundred metres. As soon as we could leave our shelter, we ran into the woods, hoping to put a safe distance between us and the enemy. But the airmen saw us and went after us. The leaves hid us. As they did not know exactly where we were, they aimed their machine-guns in the direction they thought we were travelling. We heard the bullets ripping through branches, and the sinister sound of splintering wood. The *milicianos* and I followed the flight patterns of the aeroplanes; and we made a crazy journey through the trees, trying to avoid them. Meanwhile women, children and old men were falling in heaps, like flies, and everywhere we saw lakes of blood.

I saw an old peasant standing alone in a field: a machine-gun bullet killed him. For more than an hour these eighteen planes, never more than a few hundred metres in altitude, dropped bomb after bomb on Guernica. The sound of the explosions and of the crumbling houses cannot be imagined. Always they traced on the air the same tragic flight pattern, as they flew over all the streets of Guernica. Bombs fell by thousands. Later we saw the bomb craters. Some were sixteen metres in diameter and eight metres deep.

The aeroplanes left around seven o'clock, and then there came another wave of them, this time flying at an immense altitude. They were dropping incendiary bombs on our martyred city. The new bombardment lasted thirty-five minutes, sufficient to transform the town into an enormous furnace. Even then I realized the terrible purpose of this new act of vandalism. They were dropping incendiary bombs to try to convince the world that the Basques had fired their own city.

The destruction of Guernica went on altogether for two hours and forty-five minutes. When the bombing was over, the people left their shelters. I saw no one crying. Stupor was written on all their faces. Eyes fixed on Guernica, we were completely incapable of believing what we saw.

Towards dusk we could see no more than five hundred metres. Everywhere there were flames and thick black smoke. Around me people were praying and some stretched out their arms in the form of a cross, imploring mercy from Heaven.

Soon firemen arrived from Bilbao and started to work on some of the buildings which had not been bombed. We heard that the glow of the flames had been seen from Lequeitio, twenty-two kilometres away. Not even the people who went into the refuges were saved; nor the sick and wounded in the hospitals. Guernica had no anti-aircraft guns, no batteries of any kind; nor were there any machine-guns.

During the first hours of the night it was a most horrifying spectacle: men, women and children were wandering through the woods in search of their loved ones. In most cases they found only their bullet-riddled bodies.

The buildings near the Tree of Guernica, which stands on a small hill, were unharmed, but the City Hall with its valuable archives and documents was completely destroyed.

When it grew dark the flames of Guernica were reaching to the sky, and the clouds took on the colour of blood, and our faces too shone with the colour of blood.

Robert Payne, [75], pp. 223–4.

DOCUMENT 13   **WOMEN IN THE CIVIL WAR**

Republican Spain

(a) As long as any woman is kept as an object and is prevented from developing her personality, prostitution, in fact, continues to exist.

Mercedes Comaposada, editor, *Mujeres Libres* (December 1936), R. Fraser, [126], p. 285.

(b) Prostitution presents a problem of moral, economic and social character which cannot be resolved juridically. Prostitution will be abolished when sexual relations are liberalised; when Christian and bourgeois morality is transformed; when women have professions and social opportunities to secure their livelihood and that of their children; when society is established in such a way that no one remains excluded; when society can be organised to secure life and rights for all human beings.

Federica Montseny, CNT Minister of Health and Social Welfare, R. Fraser, [126], p. 285.

Francoist Spain

(c) The good National-Syndicalist State rests on the family. It will be strong if the woman is healthy, fecund, hard-working and happy, with the windows of her home and soul open to the sweet imperial dawn that the sun of the Falange is bringing us.

Azul (editorial on 2nd National Council of the women's section of the Falange, February 1938, R. Fraser, [126], p. 309.

(d) What we shall never do is put women in competition with men, because women will never succeed in equalling men; if they try, women will lose the elegance and grace necessary for a life together with men.

Pilar Primo de Rivera (sister to José Antonio, head of the women's section of the Falange), R. Fraser, [126], p. 309.

(e) The Margaritas of Tafalla
Solemnly promise on the Sacred Heart of Jesus
1. To observe modesty in dress: long sleeves, high necks, skirts to the ankle, blouses full at the chest.
2. To read no novels, newspapers or magazines, to go to no cinema or theatre, without ecclesiastical licence.
3. Neither publicly nor in private to dance dances of this century but to study and learn the old dances of Navarre and Spain.
4. Not to wear makeup as long as the war lasts.

R. Fraser, [126], p. 309.

DOCUMENT 14   THE CHURCH AND THE CRUSADE – AN
ALTERNATIVE VIEW

(a) A crusade? Ludicrous. Who could believe that generals, whom we
knew were not believers when the war started, were now fighting a
religious crusade? We tried to raise ourselves above this sort of thing.
Our only thought was the hurt being done to the faithful by a war
we had neither started nor provoked.

Father José Maria Basabilotra, a Basque priest, R. Fraser, [126], p. 417.

(b) From the start the capitalists were on Franco's side. Religion doesn't
reject capitalists; but when it is they who rush to the defence of
religion, then all I can say is that Jesus Christ knew what to make of
it. The Basque people, who are probably more Catholic than any
other in the peninsula, were totally opposed to the concept of a
crusade. To maintain that defence of religion was the cause of war is
an untruth.

Father Luis Echebarria, religious director of the Federation of Basque
Schools, R. Fraser, [126], p. 417.

(c) Very soon the majority of us clergy withdrew. The reason was the
assassinations. They were totally unjustifiable. Even worse, they were
being ordered and condoned, if not actually carried out, by people
who declared the uprising a crusade, who came out wearing religious
insignia. On the other side, it may have been worse, but there the
assassinations weren't being carried out in the name of religion.

Father José Fernandez, a parish priest in Vallodolid, R. Fraser, [126],
p. 417.

DOCUMENT 15   FRANCO'S DICTA

(a) *October 1 1936 – on the occasion of his investiture as Jefe del
Estado.*

Our work requires sacrifices from everyone, principally from those
who have more in the interests of those who have nothing. We will
ensure that there is no home without light or a Spaniard without
bread.

Paul Preston, [155], p. 186.

(b) *On December 1936, Don Juan de Borbón, heir to the throne, wrote
to Franco offering his services. Franco's answer is an example of
Franco at his most oleaginous.*

It would have given me great pleasure to accede to your request, so Spanish and so legitimate, to fight in our navy for the cause of Spain. However, the need to keep you safe would not permit you to live as a simple officer since the enthusiasm of some and the officiousness of others would stand in the way of such noble intentions. Moreover, we have to take into account the fact that the place you occupy in the dynastic order and the obligations which arise from that impose upon us all, and demand of you the sacrifice of desires which are as patriotic as they are nobly and deeply felt, in the interests of the Patria. ... It is not possible for me to follow the dictates of my soldier's heart and to accept your offer.

Paul Preston, [155], p. 210.

(c) *On March 31 1937 the Condor Legion attacked the small Basque town of Durango. The aerial and artillery bombardment killed in all 258 civilians. Commenting on this attack, Franco explained his purpose.*

Others might think that when my aircraft bomb red cities I am making a war like any other, but that is not so. My generals and I are Spaniards and we suffer in fulfilling the duty which the Patria has assigned to us but we must go on fulfilling it ... we must carry out the necessarily slow task of redemption and pacification, without which the military occupation will be largely useless. The moral redemption of the occupied zones will be long and difficult because in Spain the roots of anarchism are old and deep.

Paul Preston, [155], p. 241.

DOCUMENT 16   **EPITAPH FOR SPAIN**

In the 1930s, few British poets remained unaffected by the war in Spain. Some, like John Cornford, died there in the International Brigade. Others, such as Roy Fuller and Louis McNeice, wrote of what Spain came to mean for their generation.

(a) Times of War and Revolution

The years successively reveal the true
Significance of all the casual shapes
Shown by the atlas. What we scarcely knew
Becomes an image haunting as a face;
Each picture rising from a neglected place
To form the dial of our cursor hopes,
As that undreamt-of frontier slowly writhes
Along the wishes of explosive lives.

The pages char and turn. Our memories fail.
What emotions shook us in our youth
Are unimaginable as the truth
Our middle years pursue. And only pain
Of some disquieting vague variety gnaws,
Seeing a boy trace out a map of Spain.

Roy Fuller, quoted in Valentine Cunningham, *The Penguin Book of Spanish Civil War Verse*, p. 458.

(b) From Autumn Journal

And I remember Spain
   At Easter ripe as an egg for revolt and ruin
Though for a tripper the rain
   Was worse than the surly or the worried or the haunted faces
With writings on the walls –
   Hammer and sickle, Boicot, Viva, Muerra;
   ...
With slovenly soldiers, nuns,
   And peeling posters from the last elections
Promising bread and guns
   Or an amnesty or another
Order or else the old
   Glory veneered and varnished
As if veneer could hold
   The rotten guts and crumbled bones together.
   ...
And the day before we left
   We saw the mob in flower at Algeciras
Outside a toothless door, a church bereft
Of its images and its aura.
And at La Linea while
   The night put miles between us and Gibraltar
We heard the blood-lust of a drunkard pile
   His heaven high with curses,
And next day took the boat
   For home, forgetting Spain, not realising
That Spain would soon denote
   Our grief, our aspirations;
Not knowing that our blunt
   Ideals would find their whetstone, that our spirit
Would find its frontier on the Spanish front,
   Its body in a rag-tag army.

Louis McNeice, quoted in Valentine Cunningham, *The Penguin Book of Spanish Civil War Verse*, pp. 453–6.

POLITICAL PERSONALITIES

Alcalá Zamora, Niceto (1877–1949) Catholic politician and landowner, led Republican government in 1931, then became President until 1936.

Araquistain, Luis (1886–1959) Marxist theoretician in PSOE.

Azaña, Manuel (1880–1940) Prime Minister in liberal government 1931–33, Prime Minister after Popular Front electoral victory and then President until 1939.

Besteiro, Julián (1870–1940) Professor of Philosophy at Madrid University, leading socialist thinker, member of Casado government in 1939.

Calvo Sotelo, José (1893–1936) Monarchist politician, leader of Renovación Española until his murder in July 1936.

Casado, Colonel Segismundo (1893–1968) Leader of coup against Negrín in 1939.

Durruti, Buenaventura (1896–1936) FAI activist, most notorious in Spain; killed leading Durruti militia column before Madrid (November 1936).

Franco, General Francisco (1892–1975) 'Africanista'; commander of Army of Africa and therefore key figure in Rising; Head of State in Nationalist Spain and subsequently dictator of Spain at end of war.

Gil Robles, José Maria (1901–80) CEDA leader, suspected by Left of planning authoritarian regime, aided 1936 Rising with CEDA funds.

Giral, José (1880–1962) Professor of Chemistry at Madrid University; Liberal Prime Minister in 1936.

Largo Caballero, Francisco (1869–1946) UGT and PSOE leader; Minister of Labour 1931–33; Prime Minister 1936–37.

Miaja, General José (1878–1958) Republican commander, Madrid; President of Casado's National Council in 1939.

Mola, General Emilio (1887–1937) 'Africanista', organiser of Military Rising: possible rival to Franco until his death in air crash.

Negrín, Juan (1889–1956) Professor of Physiology, Madrid University; Prime Minister May 1937–March 1939.

Nin, Andrés (1892–1937) founder of POUM; murdered by Soviet agents after May Days 1937.

Prieto, Indalecio (1883–1962) Socialist Minister 1931–33 and 1936–38; leader of moderate socialists.

Primo de Rivera, José Antonio (1903–36) son of General Primo de Rivera (Andalusian landowner and Spanish dictator from 1923 to 1930); founder of Falange; executed at Alicante in November 1936.

Queipo de Llano, General Gonzalo (1875–1951) 'Africanista'; ruler of Seville after Rising; responsible for purging of Andalusia.

Sanjurjo, General José (1887–1936) 'Africanista'; organised unsuccessful military coup (*sanjurjada*) in 1932, headed Rising in 1936 but killed in air crash.

GLOSSARY AND ABBREVIATIONS

Acción Nacional A Catholic propaganda and political group, changed name to *Acción Popular* in 1932, nucleus of CEDA.

africanista Officer who had made his career in the Moroccan campaigns.

alzamiento The Military Rising.

Bloque Nacional Militantly anti-parliamentary political group, founded in 1934 by Calvo Sotelo.

braceros Agricultural day labourers.

caballeristas The Largo Caballero wing of the socialists.

camisa nueva 'New shirt', a recent Falangist convert.

camisa vieja 'Old shirt', a Falangist from the early days.

Carlists Traditional Church–King party, with nineteenth-century roots and based mainly in Navarre. The Carlists advocated an autocratic monarchy.

Caudillo The Leader or Head of State – General Franco.

CEDA Confederación Española de Derechas Autónomas – Spain's major right-wing group, led by Gil Robles.

cedista CEDA supporter.

CNT Confederación Nacional del Trabajo – the anarcho-syndicalist trade union.

Cortes The Spanish Parliament, comprising 473 deputies.

CTV Corpo Truppe Volontarie – Fascist Italy's forces in Spain.

dictadura A military autocracy.

División Azul The Blue Division, Spanish volunteers who fought on the Russian front.

FAI Federación Anarquista Ibérica – the militant revolutionary wing of the anarchist movement.

faísta FAI member.

Falange Spanish Fascist organisation founded by José Antonio in 1933.

Falange Española Tradicionalista y de las Juntas de Ofensiva Nacional-Sindicalista The state party, headed by Franco, set up in 1937.

fueros Local liberties.

grupo de afinidad A cell of *faístas*, normally ten or less.

HOAC Hermandades obreras de Acción Católica – working-class Catholic societies, influential under Franco, which came to be politically active defenders of workers' rights.

incontrolados Faísta extremists.

JAP Juventud de Acción Popular – CEDA's youth movement.

Jefe Nacional The Chief – the title used by José Antonio (and then General Franco) as head of the Falange.

JONS Juntas de Ofensiva Nacional-Sindicalista – a fascist group founded by Ramiro Ledesma Ramos in 1931, merged with Falange in 1934 with joint name: Falange Española de las Juntas de Ofensiva Nacional-Sindicalista.

latifundios The great landed estates, found mainly in southern Spain.

limpieza Political cleansing carried out by Franco.

minifundios Pocket-handkerchief holdings, typical of Galicia.

Movimiento The Movement, the blander name given to the Falange as Francoism changed direction.

paseo The Spanish equivalent of the American gangster term 'to take someone for a ride'.

patria chica This phrase conveys the intense localism of Spanish life; the nearest equivalent would be 'my backyard' or 'my patch'.

PCE Partido Comunista de España – the Spanish Communist Party.

POUM Partido Obrero de Unificación Marxista – a Marxist Socialist Party, founded in 1935, and independent of the PCE and the Stalinists.

prietistas The Prieto wing of the socialists.

pronunciamiento Officers' revolt.

PSOE Partido Socialista Obrero Español – the socialist party.

PSUC Partido Socialista Unificado de Cataluña – a pro-Stalin Marxist party founded in July 1936 in Catalonia.

Renovación Española Monarchist political party.

requetés Carlist militia.

sanjurjada 1932 Rising named after its prime mover, General Sanjurjo.

SIM Servicio de Investigación Militar – the Republican secret police, founded after the fall of Largo Caballero's government in May 1937.

UGT Unión General de Trabajadores – the socialist trade union organisation.

UME Unión Militar Española – right-wing officers' organisation.

UMRA Unión Militar Republicana Antifascista – junior officer group in opposition to UME.

BIBLIOGRAPHY

THE BACKGROUND

1   Alba, Victor, *Catalonia*, C. Hurst, 1975
2   Brenan, Gerald, *The Spanish Labyrinth*, Cambridge University Press, 1943
3   Carr, Raymond, *Spain 1808–1939*, Oxford University Press, 1966
4   Carr, Raymond, *Modern Spain*, Oxford University Press, 1980
5   Delzell, C. M., *Mediterranean Fascism*, Macmillan, 1971
6   Fontana, Josep, and Nadal, Jordi, *Spain 1914–1970* in Fontana Economic History of Europe: Contemporary Economics, Part Two, ed. C. M. Cipolla, Fontana, 1976
7   Fraser, Ronald, *The Pueblo, A Mountain Village on the Costa del Sol*, Allen Lane, 1973
8   Herr, Richard, *An Historical Essay on Modern Spain*, University of California Press, 1974
9   Malefakis, E. E., *Agrarian Reform and Peasant Revolution in Spain*, Yale University Press, 1970.
10 Martinez Alier, Juan, *Labourers and Landowners in Southern Spain*, Oxford University Press, 1971
11 Meaker, Gerald, *The Revolutionary Left in Spain, 1914–23*, Stanford University Press, 1974
12 Mendizábal, Alfred, *The Martyrdom of Spain*, Geoffrey Bles, 1938
13 Nadal, Jordi, *Spain 1830–1914*, in Fontana Economic History of Europe: The Emergence of Industrial Societies, Part Two, ed. C. M. Cipolla, Fontana, 1973
14 Oliveira, Ramón, *Politics, Economics and Men of Modern Spain*, Gollancz, 1946
15 Payne, Stanley G., *Politics and the Military in Modern Spain*, Stanford University Press, 1967
16 Payne, Stanley G., *History of Basque Nationalism*, Nevada University Press, 1975
17 Pitt-Rivers, J. A., *The People of the Sierra*, Weidenfeld & Nicolson, 1954
18 Rama, Carlos, *La crisis española del siglo XX*, Fondo de Cultura Económica, Mexico, 1960
19 Sánchez, Jóse M., *Reform and Reaction*, University of North Carolina Press, 1964

20   Sánchez-Albornoz, Nicolás, *España hace un siglo: una economia dual*, Alianza, Madrid, 1972

21   Shaw, Rafael, *Spain from Within*, T. Fisher Unwin, 1910

22   Thomas, Hugh (ed.), *José Antonio Primo de Rivera, Selected Writings*, Cape, 1972

23   Trend, J. B., *The Origins of Modern Spain*, Cambridge University Press, 1934

24   Ullman, Joan C., *The Tragic Week*, Harvard University Press, 1968

THE SECOND REPUBLIC

25   Alexander, Martin S. and Graham, Helen, *The French and Spanish Popular Fronts: Comparative Perspectives*, Cambridge University Press, 1988

26   Ben-Ami, Shlomo, *The Origins of the Second Republic in Spain*, Oxford University Press, 1978

27   Ben-Ami, Shlomo, 'The Republican take-over: prelude to inevitable catastrophe', in Preston, Paul (ed), [77]

28   Blázquez, José Martin, *I Helped to Build an Army*, Secker & Warburg, 1939

29   Blinkhorn, Martin, *Carlism and Crisis in Spain 1931– 9*, Cambridge University Press, 1939

30   Blinkhorn, Martin, 'The Basque Ulster: Navarre and the Basque autonomy question under the Spanish Second Republic', *Historical Journal*, vol. XVII, no 3. (1974), pp. 593–613

31   Grossi, Manuel, *L'Insurrection des Asturies*, EDI, Paris, 1972

32   Jackson, Gabriel, *The Spanish Republic and the Civil War 1931–39*, Princeton University Press, 1965

33   Lynam, Stephen, ' "Moderate" conservatism and the Second Republic: the case of Valencia', in Blinkhorn, Martin (ed.), [49]

34   Manning, Leah, *What I Saw in Spain*, Gollancz, 1935

35   Payne, Stanley G., *Falange*, Stanford University Press, 1961

36   Preston, Paul, *The Coming of the Spanish Civil War*, Macmillan, 1978

37   Preston, Paul, 'Alfonsist monarchism and the coming of the Spanish Civil War', *Journal of Contemporary History*, vol. 7, July and October 1972

38   Preston, Paul, 'Spain's October Revolution and the rightist grasp for power', *Journal of Contemporary History*, vol. 10, October 1975

39   Preston, Paul, 'The origins of the socialist schism in Spain 1917–31', *Journal of Contemporary History*, vol. 12, January 1977

40   Preston, Paul, 'The "Moderate" right and the undermining of the Spanish Republic 1931–3', *European Studies Review*, vol. 3, October 1973

41   Preston, Paul (ed.), *Leviatán*, 4 vols, Kraus Reprint, 1974

42   Robinson, Richard A. H., *The Origins of Franco's Spain*, David &
     Charles, 1970
43   Shubert, A., 'The epic failure: the Asturian Revolution of October
     1934', in Preston, Paul (ed.), [77]
44   Shubert, A., *A Social History of Modern Spain*, Unwin Hyman, 1990
45   Tusell Gómez, Xavier, 'The Popular Front elections in Spain 1936',
     in Payne, Stanley G., *Politics and Society in 20th century Spain*,
     New Viewpoints, 1976
46   Thomas, Hugh, 'The hero in the empty room – José Antonio and
     Spanish fascism', *Journal of Contemporary History*, vol. 1, 1966
47   Vincent, Mary, 'The politicisation of Catholic women in Salamanca',
     in Lannon, Frances and Preston, Paul (eds), [71]

THE CIVIL WAR

48   Blinkhorn, Martin, 'Anglo-American historians and the Second
     Spanish Republic – the emergence of a new orthodoxy', *European
     Studies Review*, no. 1, January 1973
49   Blinkhorn, Martin (ed.), *Spain in Crisis 1931–9: Democracy and its
     Enemies*, Sage, London, 1986
50   Bolloten, Burnett, *The Spanish Revolution*, University of North
     Carolina Press, 1979
51   Broué, Pierre, and Témime, Emile, *The Revolution and Civil War in
     Spain*, Faber, 1970
52   Carr, E. H., *The Comintern and the Spanish Civil War*, Macmillan,
     1984
53   Carr, Raymond (ed.), *The Republic and the Civil War*, Weidenfeld &
     Nicolson, 1977
54   Carr, Raymond, *The Civil War in Spain 1936–39*, Weidenfeld &
     Nicolson, 1986
55   Casado, S., *The Last Days of Madrid*, Peter Davies, 1939
56   Cattell, David, *Communism and the Spanish Civil War*, University of
     California Press, 1955
57   Colodny, Robert, *The Struggle for Madrid*, Paine-Whitman, 1958
58   Coverdale, J. F., *Italian Intervention in the Spanish Civil War*,
     Princeton University Press, 1975
59   Eby, Cecil, *Between the Bullet and the Lie*, Reinhart & Winston,
     New York, 1969
60   Eby, Cecil, *The Siege of the Alcazar*, Bodley Head, 1966
61   Edwards, Jill, *The British Government and the Spanish Civil War
     1936–9*, Macmillan, 1979
62   Ellwood, Sheelagh, 'Falange Española, 1933–39: from Fascism to
     Francoism', in Blinkhorn, Martin (ed.), [49]
63   Esenwein, George and Shubert, Adrian, *Spain at War*, Longman,
     1995

64   Fischer, Louis, *Men and Politics*, Duell, Sloan & Pearce, New York, 1941

65   Fraser, Ronald, 'The popular experience of war and revolution', in Paul Preston (ed.), [77]

66   Gibson, Ian, *The Death of Lorca*, Allen, 1973

67   Harper, Glenn T., *German Economic Policy in Spain during the Spanish Civil War*, Mouton, 1967

68   Hills, George, *The Battle for Madrid*, Vintage Books, 1976

69   Hubbard, John R., 'How Franco financed his war', *Journal of Modern History*, Vol. 25, December 1953

70   Krivitsky, Walter, *I was Stalin's Agent*, Hamish Hamilton, 1963

71   Lannon, Frances and Preston, Paul (eds) *Elites and Power in 20th Century Spain*, Oxford University Press, 1990

72   Madariaga, S., *Spain: A Modern History*, Cape 1946

73   Mangini, Shirley, *Memories of Resistance*, Yale University Press, 1995

74   Monteath, Peter, 'Guernica reconsidered: fifty years of evidence', *War and Society*, vol. 5, no. 1, 1987

75   Payne, Robert, *The Civil War in Spain*, Secker & Warburg, 1963

76   Payne, Stanley G., *The Spanish Revolution*, Weidenfeld & Nicolson, 1970

77   Preston, Paul, (ed.) *Revolution and War in Spain 1931–39*, Methuen, 1984

78   Preston, Paul, *The Spanish Civil War 1936–9*, Weidenfeld & Nicolson, 1986

79   Sanchez, José M., *The Spanish Civil War as a Religious Tragedy*, University of Notre Dame Press, Indiana, 1987

80   Smyth, Denis, ' "We are with you": solidarity and self-interest in Soviet policy towards Republican Spain', in Corish, Patrick (ed.), *Radicals, Rebels, and Establishments*, Appletree Press, Belfast, 1983

81   Smyth, Denis, 'Reflex reaction: Germany and the onset of the Spanish Civil War', in Preston, Paul (ed.), [77]

82   Southworth, Herbert, *Guernica*, University of California Press, 1977

83   Stansky, Peter, and Abrahams, William, *Journey to the Frontier*, W. W. Norton, New York, 1966

84   Steer, G. L., *The Tree of Gernika*, Hodder & Stoughton, 1938

85   Thomas, Hugh, *The Spanish Civil War*, 3rd edn, Penguin, 1977

86   Thomas, Gordon, and Morgan-Witts, Max, *The Day Guernica Died*, Hodder & Stoughton, 1975

87   Traina, Richard P., *American Diplomacy and the Spanish Civil War*, Indiana University Press, 1968

88   Trotsky, Leon, *The Spanish Revolution (1931–39)*, Pathfinder Press, New York, 1973

89   Viñas, Ángel, *La Alemania Nazi y el 18 de julio*, Alianza Editorial, Madrid, 1974

90   Viñas, Ángel, 'The financing of the Spanish Civil War', in Preston, Paul (ed.), [77]

91 Viñas, Ángel, 'Gold, the Soviet Union and the Spanish Civil War', in Blinkhorn, Martin (ed.), [49]

92 Watkins, K., *Britain Divided*, Nelson, 1963

93 Watt, D. C., 'Soviet aid to the Republic', *Slavonic and East European Review*, no. 1, June 1960

94 Weintraub, Stanley, *The Last Great Cause: The Intellectuals and the Spanish Civil War*, Allen, 1968

SPANISH ANARCHISM

95 Whealey, Robert H., 'How Franco financed his war', in Blinkhorn, Martin (ed.), [49]

96 Whealey, Robert H., *Hitler and Spain: The Nazi Role in the Spanish Civil War*, University Press of Kentucky, 1989

97 Abad de Santillán, Diego, *Por qué perdimos la guerra*, Del Toro, Madrid, 1975

98 Bauer, Augustin Souchy, *With the Peasants in Aragon*, Cienfuegos, Orkney, 1982

99 Bookchin, Murray, *The Spanish Anarchists*, Free Life, New York, 1977

100 Chomsky, N., *American Power and the New Mandarins*, Penguin, 1969

101 Dolgoff, Sam, *The Anarchist Collectives*, Free Life, New York, 1974

102 Goldman, Emma, *Visions on Fire*, Commonground, New Paltz, New York, 1983

103 Hobsbawm, E. P., *Primitive Rebels*, Manchester University Press, 1959

104 Kaplan, Tamma, 'Spanish anarchism and women's liberation', *Journal of Contemporary History*, vol. 6, 1971

105 Kaplan, Tamma, *Anarchists of Andalusia 1868–1903*, Princeton University Press, Princeton, 1977

106 Kelsey, Graham, 'Anarchism in Aragon during the Second Republic: the emergence of a mass movement', in Blinkhorn, Martin (ed.), [49]

107 Leval, Gaston, *Collectives in the Spanish Revolution*, Freedom Press, 1975

108 Lorenzo, C. M., *Los anarquistas españoles y el poder*, Ruedo Ibérico, Paris, 1969

109 Mintz, Frank, *L'Autogestion dans l'Espagne révolutionnaire*, Belibaste, 1970

110 Mintz, Jerome R., *The Anarchists of Casas Viejas*, University of Chicago Press, 1982

111 Paz, Abel, *Durruti: The People Armed*, Black Rose Books, Montreal, 1976

112 Peirats, José, *Anarchists in the Spanish Revolution*, Freedom Press, 1990

113   Richards, V., *Lessons of the Spanish Revolution*, Freedom Press, 1953
114   Thomas, Hugh, 'Anarchist agrarian collectives in the Spanish Civil War', in Gilbert, Martin, *A Century of Conflict*, Hamish Hamilton, 1966
115   Woodcock, G., *Anarchism*, Penguin, 1963
116   Woodcock, G., *The Anarchist Reader*, Fontana, 1977

PERSONAL ACCOUNTS

117   Barea, Arturo, *The Forging of a Rebel*, David-Poynter, 1972
118   Bolín, Luis, *Spain, the Vital Years*, Cassell, 1967
119   Bowers, Claude, *My Mission to Spain*, Gollancz, 1954
120   Borkenau, Franz, *The Spanish Cockpit*, Faber, 1937
121   Brenan, Gerald, *Personal Record*, Cape, 1974
122   Buckley, Henry, *Life and Death of the Spanish Republic*, Hamish Hamilton, 1940
123   Campesino, El (González, Valentín), *Listen, Comrades*, Heinemann, 1952
124   Copeman, Fred, *Reason in Revolt*, Blandford Press, 1948
125   Fraser, Ronald, *In Hiding*, Allen Lane, 1972
126   Fraser, Ronald, *The Blood of Spain*, Allen Lane, 1979
127   Gellhorn, Martha, *The Face of War*, Hart-Davis, 1969
128   Gurney, Jason, *Crusade in Spain*, Faber, 1974
129   Ibarruri, Dolores, *They Shall Not Pass*, Lawrence & Wishart 1967
130   Kemp, Peter, *Mine were of Trouble*, Cassell, 1957
131   Knoblaugh, H. Edward, *Correspondent in Spain*, Sheed & Ward, 1939
132   Maisky, Ivan, *Spanish Notebooks*, Hutchinson, 1966
133   Mera, Cipriano, *Guerra, exilio y cárcel de un anarcosindicalista*, Ruedo Ibérico, Paris, 1976
134   de la Mora, Constance, *In Place of Splendour*, Michael Joseph, 1940
135   Orwell, George, *Homage to Catalonia*, Penguin, 1962
136   Pérez López, Francisco, *Dark and Bloody Ground*, Little Brown, Toronto, 1970
137   Regler, Gustav, *The Owl of Minerva*, Hart Davis, 1959
138   Romilly, Esmond, *Boadilla*, Macdonald, 1971
139   Sender, Ramón, *The War in Spain*, Faber, 1937
140   Toynbee, Philip, *The Distant Drum*, Sidgwick & Jackson, 1976
141   Wintringham, Tom, *English Captain*, Faber, 1939

FRANCO SPAIN

142   Alba, Victor, *Transition in Spain*, Transaction Books, New Brunswick, 1978
143   Blaye, Edouard de, *Franco and the Politics of Spain*, Penguin, 1976

144 Carr, Raymond, and Fusi, Juan Pablo, *Spain: Dictatorship to Democracy*, Allen & Unwin, 1979

145 Crozier, Brian, *Franco*, Eyre & Spottiswoode, 1967

146 Ellwood, Sheelagh M., *Franco*, Longman, 1993

147 Gallo, Max, *Spain under Franco*, Allen & Unwin, 1973

148 Hills, George, *Franco, the Man and his Nation*, Robert Hale, 1967

149 Medhurst, Kenneth, *Government in Spain*, Pergamon Press, 1973

150 Muggeridge, Malcolm (ed.), *Ciano's Diplomatic Papers*, Odhams, 1948

151 Payne, Stanley G., *The Franco Regime*, University of Wisconsin Press, 1987

152 Preston, Paul, *Spain in Crisis*, Harvester Press, 1976

153 Preston, Paul, *The Triumph of Democracy in Spain*, Methuen, 1986

154 Preston, Paul, *The Politics of Revenge: Fascism and the Military in 20th Century Spain*, Unwin Hyman, 1990

155 Preston, Paul, *Franco*, Fontana, 1993

156 Welles, Benjamin, *The Gentle Anarchy*, Pall Mall Press, 1965

INDEX

Abad de Santillán, Diego, 16, 30, 57
Accidentalism, 14, 34
Acción Nacional (Acción Popular), 2, 6, 25
Africanistas, 2, 10, 34, 48, 65, 93
Agrarian reform, 11–13, 17, 28, 69
Agrarian Reform Bill, 13
agriculture, 5, 6
air attacks, 42, 44, 72, 75
Air Force, 39
Alcalá Zamora, Niceto, 8, 9, 17, 33
Alcázar, 41
Alfonso XIII, 2, 3, 10, 21
Alfonsists, 19, 20
Alto de León Pass, 41
Alzamiento, 70
Anarchists, 5, 6, 28, 54, 65, 101, Doc. 3
Anarcho-syndicalists, 5, 28
Arnedo, 14
Andalusia, 5, 11, 21, 29, 37, 39, 64, 92, 101
Anti-clericalism, 9, 55, 56
Anti-Comintern Pact, (1939), 80, 96
Anti-Fascist Militia Committee, 55, 57
Aragon, 28, 39, 55, 57, 72, 91
Araquistain, Luis, 8, 26
Army, 1, 9, 10, 14, 15, 16, 26, 34, 35, 38, 39, 91, 99
Army of Africa, 39, 41, 48, 67, 91
Articles of the Constitution, (1931), 9
Asensio, Torrado, General, 45

Assault Guards, 14, 18, 35, 38
Asturian Rising, 18, 19, 22, 25, 26, 27, 28, 42, 89, 90, Doc 1
Azaña, Manuel, 3, 8, 9, 10, 13, 14, 15, 16, 18, 20, 24, 26, 27, 28, 29, 30, 32, 33, 35, 73, 98

Badajoz massacres, 63, 73
Balearics, 35, 38
Bakunin, Mikhail, 5
Barcelona, 18, 38, 43, 64, 76, 86, 87, 90, 91
Barcelona May Days, 58, 59, 60, 74, 91, Doc. 11
Basque Provinces, 4, 5, 40, 54, 64, 71, 74, 79, 91,100
Belchite, 83, 93
Ben-Ami, Shlomo, 13
Bernanos, Georges, 64, Doc. 6
Besteiro, Julián, 17, 20, 73, 87, 88
Bilbao, 39, 43, 71, 73
Blinkhorn, Martin, 21
Bloque Nacional, 21
Blum, Léon, 50, 51, 52, 75
Bolín, Luis, 37, 49
Bolloten, Burnett, 60, 62, 80, 85
British Battalion of the International Brigades, 45, 74, 82, 83
Broué, Pierre and Témime, Emile, 28, 59
Brunete, 72, 74, 75, 77, 80, 83, 93
Buckley, Henry, 43

Caballeristas, 30, 32
Cabanellas, General Miguel, 67
Cádiz, 37, 44

Calvo Sotelo, Jose, 20, 21, 23, 24, 25, 31, 36
Campesino, El, 74, 75
Canaries, 37
Carlists, 1, 2, 19, 20, 26, 27, 28, 31, 35, 65, 68, 78
Carr, Raymond, 34, 38, 43, 75, 86, 92
Casado, Colonel Segismundo, 87
Casals, Pablo, 64, 101
Casares Quiroga, Santiago, 16, 33, 40
Castile, 10, 12, 39, 101
Castilblanco, 14
Castillo, Lieut. José, 35
Catalan: language, 4, 54, 98
Catalan Statute, 11
Catalonia, 4, 5, 6, 17, 18, 29, 38, 39, 40, 41, 54, 55, 56, 57, 58, 59, 63, 72, 76, 80, 86, 91
Caudillo, 69, 96
Caudwell, Christopher, 46
CEDA, 2, 15, 17, 18, 19, 21, 24, 25, 27, 31, 32, 34, 35
Cedistas, 25, 26
Chomsky, Noam, 59, 86
Church, 1, 9, 14, 20, 64, 69, 70, 93, 99, 100
CNT, 6, 16, 20, 23, 28, 29, 34, 38, 39, 40, 45, 55, 58, 59, 61, 66, 75, 86
Collective Letter, (1937), 70
Collectives, 11, 54, 55, 57
Comintern, 26, 27, 58, 77
Communist Fifth Regiment, 42, 61, 82
Companys, Luis, 17, 18, 98
Concordat (1851), 3, 4
Condor Legion, 44, 46, 72, 75, 80
Conscription, 10, 49, 74
Constitution of 1812, 3
Córdoba, 21, 37
Cortes, 8, 9, 13, 20, 31, 33, 65, 85, 100, 102
CTV, 45, 46, 80
Cuenca, 24, 33

Decree of Unification, (1937), 68
Dictadura, 2, 20, 28

División Azul, 96
Durruti, Buenaventura, 16, 42, 61, 82, 90

Ebro offensive, 71, 76, 83, 87
Eden, Sir Anthony, 50, 73
Edwards, Jill, 49, 53
Elections, (1931, 1933, 1936), 2, 8, 17, 21, 24, 31
Electoral system, 31
emigration, 7
Extremadura, 12, 14, 29, 34, 39, 80, 92

FAI, 16, 61, *Doc. 3(b)*
Falange Española, 20, 21, 22, 23, 24, 26, 27, 31, 34, 35, 66, 67, 68, 78, 92, *Doc. 4*
Falange Española Tradicionalista, 68, 98, 101
Fanjul, General Joaquín, 32, 34, 35, 38
Ferdinand VII, 2
Ferrer, Francisco, 3
Foreign Legion, 18, 45
Foreign Aid,
  German, 44, 52, 77, 79, 80, 95
  Italian, 46, 49, 51, 52, 77, 79, 80
  Soviet, 43, 44, 52, 77, 95
France, 49, 50, 51, 52, 74, 75, 77, 81, 96, 97, 98
Fraser, Ronald, 55, 64, 99
Franco, General Francisco, 41, 42, 43, 44, 45, 46, 47, 48, 54, 56, 61, 65, 67, 68, 69, 70, 71, 72, 73, 74, 75, 77, 79, 81, 83, 87, 88, 91, 93, 96, 97, *Doc. 15*
Fueros, 10

Galicia, 4, 11, 39, 42, 101
Gal, General, 82
García Lorca, Federico, 64
García Oliver, Juan, 56
Generalitat, 17, 38, 55, 57, 58
Gender relations, 93, 94, *Doc. 13*
'Generation of 98', 8, 64
Germany, 49, 51, 52, 53, 77, 79, 80, 81, 99
Gibraltar, 53, 81, 96

Gibson, Ian, 64
Gil Robles, José Maria, 15, 16, 17, 19, 20, 25, 30, 31, 32, 33, 34, 35, 89
Giner, Francisco, 3, 64
Giral, José, 40, 54, 56, 61, 78
Goded, General Manuel, 15, 18, 34, 38, 41, 91
Goicoechea, Antonio, 21
Granada, 21
Great Britain, 49, 50, 51, 53, 74, 79, 81, 96, 98
Guadalajara, 46, 47, 51, 55, 75, 77, 80
Guernica, 72, 73, *Doc. 12*

Hedilla, Manuel, 67, 68
Hendaye, 81
Herrera, Angel, 14
Hidalgo, Diego, 18
Hills, George, 43
Hitler, Adolf, 19, 25, 48, 53, 67, 80, 81, 89, 91, 95
HOAC, 100
Huesca, 28, 74

Ibarruri, Dolores, 29, 98
INC, 101
Incontrolados, 16, 59
Inquisition, 2
Institute of Agrarian Reform, 13
Institute of Free Education, 3
International Brigades, 42, 43, 44, 46, 62, 71, 74, 77, 80, 81, 82, 83, 84, 93, *Doc. 8*
Italy, 51, 52, 77, 79, 80, 81, 99

Jaén, 12
Jackson, Gabriel, 59, 60
JAP, 15
Jarama, 45, 46, 82, 83
Jefe Nacional, 23, 24, 67, 68
Jérez, 15, 21, 37
JONS, 22
Junkers, 41, 48

KGB, 52
Kindelán, General Afredo, 42
Knoblaugh, H. E. 43
Konsomol, 78

Labour Charter, (1938), 68
Laboreo forzoso, 12
Largo Caballero, Francisco, 11, 17, 19, 26, 27, 30, 32, 33, 40, 42, 45, 56, 57, 59, 60, 61, 62, 63, 72, 77, 78, 80, 84, 85, 86, 90, 92, 98
Latifundios, 5, 11
Law of Political Responsibilities, (1939), 89, 98
Ledesma, Ramiro, 22
Left Republicans, 8, 27, 28, 29
Lerroux, Alejandro, 8, 17, 18, 19, 20, 27
Limpieza, e 45, 98
Lister, General Enrique, 74, 75
López, Pérez, 76, 83

Macià, Colonel Francisco, 11
Madrid, 38, 41, 42, 43, 44, 46, 47, 63, 64, 71, 77, 87, 88, *Doc. 10*
Majorca, 51, 64
Málaga, 39, 44, 45, 73, 80, 90
Malefakis, E. E., 12
Mancomunidad, 4
Martínez Barrio, Diego, 18, 28, 40
Marxism, 1, 24, 100, 102
Maura, Miguel, 8, 9, 18
Melilla, 37
Mexico, 52
Miaja, General José, 42, 45, 87
Military Rising, 2, 19, 33, 37, 48, 65, 67, 81, 90, 93, *Doc. 2*
Militias, 38, 39, 40, 43, 54, 58, 61, 62, *Doc. 7*
Millán Astray, General José, 65
Minifundios, 11, 101
Mola, General Emilio, 24, 26, 34, 35, 40, 41, 42, 48, 67, 91
Montseney, Federica, 56, 98
Moors, 45, 46, 64, 74
Morocco, 37, 48
Moscardó, Colonel, José, 41
'Movement' (Falange), 68, 69, 99, *Doc. 4(b)*
Munich Agreement (1938), 80, 83
Mussolini, Benito, 45, 46, 48, 49, 75, 80, 89

Nadal, Jordi, 4, 7
National Council, (1937), 69
National Council, (1939), 87
National Defence Council,
(1937), 67
Navarre, 28, 29, 40, 68
Navy, 39
Negrín, Dr Juan, 60, 74, 76, 80,
85, 86, 87, 88
Nin, Andrés, 95
NKVD, 52, 85
Non-Intervention Agreement,
(1936), 50, 51, 79, 95

Ortega y Gasset, Eduardo, 8,
13
Orwell, George, 55, 59, 90
Oviedo, 18, 22, 38, 42, 59, 90

Pact of Madrid, (1953), 97
Pact of San Sebastián, (1930),
10
Pamplona, 35, 36, 40, 41
Pardo, Lorenzo, 11
Paseos, 64, *Doc. 5*
Patria chica, 4
Payne, Stanley, 15, 35, 74
PCE, 20, 29, 30, 31, 39, 58, 59,
60, 102
Peasant Federation, 57
Pestaña, Angel, 16
Picasso, Pablo, 98, 101
Political Commissars, 62, 80, 84,
93
Popular Army, 59, 61, 62, 71,
75, 92
Popular Front, 56, 61, 85
POUM, 20, 29, 30, 31, 54, 55,
58, 59, 80, 85
Preston, Paul, 21, 24, 31, 33,
45, 93
Prietistas, 23, 32, 60, 88
Prieto, Indalecio, 17, 19, 20, 23,
26, 29, 30, 32, 33, 56, 60, 80,
85, 86, 87, 90, 98
Primo de Rivera General Miguel,
2, 4, 6, 34, 68
Primo de Rivera, José Antonio,
21, 22, 23, 24, 31, 49, 66, 91,
Doc. 4

Pronunciamiento, 1, 15, 35, 37
PSOE, 6, 20, 23, 26, 27, 29, 78,
102
PSUC, 29, 58

Queipo de Llano, General
Gonzalo, 38, 45, 64, *Doc. 2(e)*

Rabassaires, 17
Rama, Carlos, 1
Radicals, 27, 32
Regulares, 18
Renovación Española, 2, 21, 23
Reparto, 5
Republican-Socialist alliance, 2,
30, 31
Republican Union, 28, 31
Requetés, 20, 35, 40
Rio Tinto, 78, 79
Roatta, General Mario, 45, 46
Robinson, Richard, A. H., 24
Rojo, General Vicente, 75, 76
Rosenberg, Marcel, 52, 56, 60
Rossi, 'Count', 64, *Doc. 6*

Salamanca, 64, 72
Sanchez-Albernoz, Nicolás, 5
Sanjurjada, (1932), 13, 15
Sanjurjo, General José, 14, 15,
35, 67, 91
Santander, 39, 73
Saragossa, 10, 28, 38, 41, 67
Segura, Cardinal Pedro, 9
Seville, 15, 39, 45
SIM, 63, 80, 84, 85
Socialists, 8, 13, 17, 18, 27, 31,
33, 56
Somosierra Pass, 41
Southworth, Herbert, 64, 73
Soviet Union, 49, 52, 60, 77, 78,
85, 90, 92
Stalin, J. V., 52, 53, 56, 61, 77,
80
Steer, G. L., 72
Serrano Suñer, Ramon, 25, 35, 67
Syndicalists, 30, 31

Términos municipales, 12
Technical Commission (1931),
12, 13

Tenerife, 35, 37
Teruel, 28, 71, 75, 76, 80, 83,
   86, 87, 93
Tetuán, 37
Texas Oil Company, 52, 84
Thomas, Hugh, 19, 33, 59, 60,
   74, 77, 82, 84, 86
Toledo, 41, 42
Treintistas, 16

UGT, 6, 20, 34, 39, 59, 66, 110
UME, 32, 34, 35, 38
Unión Militar Antifascista, 38
USA, 52, 96, 97
United Nations, 96, 97

Uribe, Vicente, 57

Valencia, 16, 26, 38, 39, 42, 43,
   44, 45, 58, 71, 72, 86
Vallodolid, 23, 41
Vinaroz, 76
Viñas, Angel, 48, 49, 78

Whealey, Robert, 79
Wolfram, 81
World War II, 81, 96, 99

Yague, Colonel Juan de, 63
Yugoslavia, 82